Beachy

family favorites

Recipes from home and bakery

First Printing   June 2013   2M
Second Printing   September 2013   3M

ISBN 978-061581526-8

For additional copies contact your local bookstore or—
Beachy's Bulk Foods
259 N County Road 200 E
Arthur, IL 61911

Layout & Design | Grace Troyer

Carlisle Printing
OF WALNUT CREEK LTD
800.927.4196 · carlisleprinting.com
Sugarcreek, Ohio 44681

Introduction

In sincere appreciation to all our friends and customers we have compiled a cookbook of our favorite recipes. In 1998 we put together a small cookbook with the recipes we used in the store and also some others. Then in 2007 when it was time to order cookbooks again, we decided to really make it a family cookbook. We had recipes of food we made in the bakery, recipes when the children were growing up, and also from each of the children's homes. Most of the grandchildren added several recipes too. Now in 2013 we are renewing our cookbook again and everyone has added some more recipes. We hope you will enjoy the new cookbook! We apologize for any errors you may find.

*We have marked the recipes that are made in the bakery with a star so you can easily find them.

May God bless you!

Levi & Katie Beachy and family
2013 – Arthur, Illinois

Table of Contents

A blessing be upon the cook,
who seeing, buys this little book,
and buying tries and tests its wares,
and testing throws away her cares,
and carefree tells her neighbor cook,
to get another "such-a-book".
May God bless you!

Thank God for Dirty Dishes

Thank God for dirty dishes
They have a tale to tell.
While others may go hungry,
We're eating very well!

With home and health and happiness,
We shouldn't make a fuss.
For by this stack of evidence,
God has been good to us!

Beatitudes for Homemakers

– Blessed is she whose daily tasks are a work of love: for her willing hands and happy heart transform duty into joyous service to all her family and God.

– Blessed is she who opens the door to welcome both stranger and well-loved friends: for gracious hospitality is a test of brotherly love.

– Blessed is she who mends both stockings and broken toys and broken hearts: for her understanding is a balm to her husband and children.

– Blessed is she who scours and scrubs: for well she knows that cleanliness is one expression of godliness.

– Blessed is she whom children love: for the love of a child is of greater value than fortune or fame.

– Blessed is she who sings in her work: for music lightens the heaviest load and brightens the dullest chore.

– Blessed is she who dusts away doubt and fear and sweeps all the cobwebs of confusion: for her faith will triumph over all adversity.

– Blessed is she who serves laughter and smiles with every meal: for her cheerfulness is an aid to mental and physical digestion.

– Blessed is she who introduces Jesus Christ to her children: for Godly sons and daughters shall be her reward.

– Blessed is she who preserves the sacredness of the Christian home: for hers is a divine trust that crowns her with dignity.

–Ella May Miller

"Come In"

Come in! But don't expect to find
All dishes done, all floors ashine:
See crumpled rugs, the toys galore
The smudged, fingerprinted door,
The little ones we shelter here
Don't thrive in spotless atmosphere:
They're more inclined to disarray
And carefree, even messy play.

Their needs are great, patience small
All day I'm at their beck and call.
It's "Mommie, come!", "Mommie, see!"
Wiggly worms and red scraped knee,
Painted pictures, blocks piled high,
My floors unshined, the days go by.
Some future day they'll flee this nest
And I at last will have a rest.
And which really matters more-
A happy child, or a polished floor?

History of Beachy's Bulk Foods

We thought our customers may be interested in knowing how our store got started. So we will try to write a little history.

In 1976 we moved to the current farm. We had decided to quit milking cows and raise hogs and have a large produce patch. After a year or so we decided to change the hoghouse into a chicken house and milk cows again. So now we had eggs and homegrown produce to sell from our front porch. Then having too many eggs we started baking for another local store, and also selling some with our eggs and produce. Things went from one thing to the next, and soon we were into wholesale baking. Several years later we built a small store and bakery beside the large farmhouse. We did a lot of wholesale baking there. After 6 years we cleared away the apple orchard north of the house, and built a new store. After several years in the new store we quit wholesale baking, as we had more than we could do. We were in that store for 17 years, then in 2003 we built a new store and turned the old store into a warehouse.

Kitchen Prayer

Bless my little kitchen, Lord

I love it's every nook

And bless me as I do my work,

Wash pots and pans and cook.

May the meals that I prepare,

Be seasoned from above,

With Thy blessings and Thy grace

But most of all, Thy love.

As we partake of earthly food

The table throw has spread

We'll not forget to "Thank Thee, Lord"

For all our daily bread.

So bless my little kitchen, Lord

And those who enter in.

May they find naught but joy and peace,

And happiness therein!

Amen

Today I must have Martha's hands, for there's so much to do. That if I miss a minute of time I never shall get through the many tasks that wait for me. And so, Dear Lord, I pray for strength and swiftness. Give to me "Martha's hands" today.

Today I must have Mary's heart. There are so many things that must be done today. Time goes by on rapid wings, and so, lest I engrossed with work should lose that better part, I pray keep me close to Thee, and give me a "Mary's heart."

– Lori C. Gooding

Breakfast

Breakfast Casserole

Jonathan Lee Miller

6 eggs   2 c. milk
ham, sausage, or bacon   6 slices bread, cubed
salt   cheese
pepper

Heat oven to 350°. Beat eggs, add ham, salt and pepper to taste. Add milk and bread cubes. Pour in pan and bake 30 minutes or until done. Put cheese slices on top.

Breakfast Casserole

Larry Allen Miller, Steven & Lorene Helmuth

6 slices bread   6–8 eggs
ham, bacon, sausage   3–3½ c. milk
2 c. shredded cheese   salt and pepper to taste

Topping:
1 c. crushed cornflakes   ¼ c. butter, melted

Arrange 6 slices of bread in 9"x13" pan. Sprinkle your choice of meat on bread. Spread the shredded cheese on top. Mix together beaten eggs, milk, salt and pepper. Pour over bread, meat, and cheese. Mix together topping and spread on top. Refrigerate overnight. Bake at 350° for 1 hour or until done.

Variation: May also add another 6 slices of bread after shredded cheese. Then pour egg mixture over all.

Breakfast Haystack

Wilmer & Sarah Beachy

biscuits	sausage links, cut up
sausage gravy	scrambled eggs
fried potatoes	cheese sauce
bacon, cut in bite-sized pieces	

Serve in order given and make a delicious haystack.

Breakfast Pizza

Abner & Sovilla Mae Zook

1 lb. bulk pork sausage	¼ c. milk
1 (8) pkg. refrigerated	½ tsp. salt
crescent rolls	dash of pepper
1 c. frozen hash browns	2 Tbsp. grated Parmesan
1 c. shredded cheddar cheese	or mozzarella cheese
5 eggs	

In a skillet, cook sausage until browned; drain off excess fat. Separate crescent dough into 8 triangles. Place in and ungreased 12" pizza pan, with points toward center. Press over bottom and up sides to form crust. Seal perforations. Spoon sausage over crust. Sprinkle with hash browns. Top with cheddar cheese. In a bowl beat eggs, milk, salt, pepper. Pour into crust. Sprinkle Parmesan over all. Bake at 375° for 25–30 min. Yield: 6–8 servings.

Note: I use pizza dough instead of crescent rolls.

Breakfast Pizza

Cheryl Rose Miller

½ lb. bacon, crumbled
2 c. shredded cheese
4 eggs

1½ c. sour cream
2 Tbsp. fresh parsley or
2 tsp. dried parsley

Bake crust (crescent rolls or pizza dough) at 425° for 5 minutes. Sprinkle bacon and cheese evenly over crust. In a bowl, beat eggs, sour cream and parsley until smooth. Pour over pizza. Bake at 425° for 20–25 minutes or until pizza is puffy and lightly browned.

Pancake Pizza

Wilmer & Sarah Beachy
Melvin & Beth Ann Beachy
Alvin & Charlene Kanagy

3 c. pancake batter
6 c. sausage gravy
12 eggs, scrambled

1 c. shredded cheese
1 lb. bacon, crumbled
maple syrup

Heat oven to 400°. Pour pancake batter in a 9"x13" greased and floured cake pan. Bake for 15 minutes or until done. Make sausage gravy and scrambled eggs. Remove pancake from oven when done and layer eggs, cheese, gravy, and sprinkle bacon on top. Serve with pancake syrup. Leftovers are always good warmed up again.

Amnor Pancakes

Raymond & Martha Beachy

1½ c. buttermilk	1 Tbsp. baking powder
3 egg yolks	½ tsp. soda
¼ c. shortening, melted	¼ tsp. salt
1½ c. sifted flour	3 egg whites, stiffly beaten

Combine buttermilk, yolks, and shortening. Sift together dry ingredients and add to other mixture; fold in egg whites.

Country Potato Pancakes

Orvan & Marilyn Miller

3 lg. potatoes, peeled (about 2 lbs.)	2 Tbsp. flour
2 eggs, slightly beaten	1 tsp. salt
1 Tbsp. grated onion	½ tsp. baking powder

Finely grate potatoes. Add rest of ingredients. In frying pan, add oil to the depth of ⅛"; heat over medium high heat. Drop pancakes into hot oil. Fry until golden on one side, then flip and fry on other side until done.

Pancakes

Robert & Dorothy Beachy

3 eggs	1¼ tsp. soda
2½ c. buttermilk	2¼ c. flour
4½ Tbsp. vegetable oil	2¼ tsp. baking powder
2¼ tsp. sugar	1¼ tsp. salt

Mix all together and fry on hot skillet.

Corny Vanilla Pancakes

Orvan & Marilyn Miller

1 c. cornmeal	1 Tbsp. sugar
1 c. wheat flour	1 egg
4 tsp. baking powder	¾ c. water
½ tsp. salt	¾ c. milk
⅓ c. wheat bran (optional)	1 tsp. vanilla

Combine dry ingredients except bran. Beat egg and add milk, water and vanilla. Stir into dry ingredients, mix. Stir in bran, if desired. Fry on hot oiled skillet. Makes about 8 pancakes.

Oatmeal Pancakes

Joseph & Melissa Beachy

2¼ c. oatmeal	2 Tbsp. honey or brown sugar
2 c. milk or water	2 egg yolks
2 tsp. baking powder	¼ c. melted butter or vegetable oil
1 tsp. soda	2 egg whites

Soak oatmeal in milk or water overnight. Next morning add baking powder, soda, honey or brown sugar, egg yolks and melted butter. Blend well. Beat egg whites until stiff, fold into batter. Grease griddle lightly.

Note: These pancakes require careful baking and flipping, but are delicious. Serve with peanut butter or choice of syrup.

Salsa Corn Cakes

Marnita Beachy

1½ c. flour
½ c. cornmeal
1 tsp. baking powder
1 tsp. salt
6 oz. cream cheese
6 eggs

1 c. milk
½ c. margarine
15 oz. frozen or canned corn
½ c. salsa
¼ c. minced onions

Mix all together and pour ¼ cup on hot greased griddle to form patties. When golden on both sides, serve with sour cream and salsa spread on top.

Waffles or Pancakes

Jonathan Miller

1 c. whole wheat flour
1 c. white flour
2 tsp. baking powder, round
2 tsp. sugar

5 Tbsp. butter or vegetable oil
¼ tsp. salt
3 eggs, separated
1½ c. milk

Sift flour, sugar, salt and baking powder together. To the well beaten egg yolks, add flour mixture alternately with milk. Add butter or vegetable oil. Last fold in stiffly beaten egg whites.

Sour Cream Waffles

Melvin & Beth Ann Beachy

6 eggs, beaten well
1½ c. sour cream
1½ c. buttermilk
½ c. vegetable oil
½ c. butter, melted

3 c. flour
4 tsp. baking powder
1 tsp. soda
2 Tbsp. sugar

Beat eggs, sour cream and milk. Add oil, butter and dry ingredients. Beat until batter is smooth and free from lumps. Bake on hot waffle iron.

Pancake Syrup

Lamar Jay Miller

1¼ c. brown sugar
¾ c. sugar
⅓ c. light syrup

1 c. water
pinch of salt

Boil 5 minutes. Remove from heat, add 1 teaspoon maple flavor.

Never Fail Syrup

Wilmer & Sarah Beachy

1 c. sugar
1 c. brown sugar
1 c. light syrup

1 c. water
pinch of salt
¼ tsp. maple flavoring

Mix together all ingredients except flavoring. Slowly bring to boil. Let boil 5 minutes. Remove from heat, then add flavoring.

Biscuit Mix

Alvin & Charlene Kanagy

9 c. flour
¼ c. baking powder
2 Tbsp. sugar

2 tsp. cream of tartar
2 tsp. salt
1½ c. shortening

Mix together by hand. Store in a tight container. To mix biscuits: Mix 3 cups mix to 1 cup milk (makes 10 biscuits). Mix 9 cups mix to 3½ cups milk (makes 30). We also like this for pizza dough.

Biscuit Mix

Orvan & Marilyn Miller

9 c. flour
2 c. shortening
⅓ c. baking powder

¼ c. sugar
2 tsp. cream of tartar
1 Tbsp. salt

Mix like pie crumbs. Store in airtight Tupperware. Keeps 6 months at room temperature. To mix biscuits: 3 cup biscuit mix and 1 cup milk. Measure mix lightly, stir in milk. Do not overmix. Knead lightly. Roll out to desired thickness. Cut and bake on cookie sheet at 450° for 10–15 minutes.

Hard-boiled eggs will peel easier if you boil them for 10 minutes. Remove from heat 5 minutes, then put in cold water and cool.

Melt in Your Mouth Biscuits

Orvan & Marilyn Miller

2 c. flour
2 tsp. baking powder
½ tsp. cream of tartar
½ tsp. salt

2 Tbsp. sugar
½ c. shortening
1 egg, unbeaten
⅔ c. milk

Mix together dry ingredients and cut in shortening until mixture resembles course crumbs. Add egg and milk. Bake at 450° for 10–15 minutes. I like to use this recipe for pizza dough too.

Sky High Biscuits

Orvan & Marilyn Miller

2 c. flour
1 c. whole wheat flour
4½ tsp. baking powder
2 Tbsp. sugar

¾ tsp. cream of tartar
¾ c. butter or margarine
1 egg, beaten
1 c. milk

In a bowl, combine dry ingredients. Cut in butter until mixture resembles course crumbs. Add egg and milk, stir quickly and briefly. Bake at 450° for 12–15 minutes. Yield: 20 biscuits.

Banana Split Muffins

Wilmer & Sarah Beachy

1½ c. flour
1 c. sugar
1 tsp. soda
½ tsp. salt

1 egg
½ c. salad dressing
3 ripe bananas, mashed
chocolate chips

Mix dry ingredients. In small bowl, beat egg, stir in dressing. Add to flour mixture; stir just until moist. Stir in bananas. Spoon into greased or paper-lined muffin pan. Sprinkle with chips on top. Bake at 300° for 25 minutes or until lightly browned.

Blueberry Muffins

Melvin & Beth Ann Beachy

½ c. buttermilk
¼ c. vegetable oil
1 egg
½ c. sugar
2 tsp. baking powder

½ tsp. salt
½ tsp. soda
1½ c. flour
1 c. fresh or frozen blueberries

Mix buttermilk, vegetable oil, egg, sugar, baking powder, salt and soda; then add flour. Add blueberries last. Line muffin pan with cupcake liners and fill ½ to ¾ full. Bake at 400°. Yield: 12 muffins.

Cappuccino Muffins

Renita Faye Helmuth

2 c. flour
¾ c. sugar
2½ tsp. baking powder
1 tsp. cinnamon
½ tsp. salt
1 c. milk

2 Tbsp. instant coffee
½ c. butter, melted
1 egg, beaten
1 tsp. vanilla
¾ c. mini chocolate chips

Espresso Spread:
4 oz. cream cheese
½ tsp. instant coffee
1 Tbsp. sugar

½ tsp. vanilla
¼ c. mini chocolate chips

In a bowl, combine flour, sugar, baking powder, cinnamon and salt. In a separate bowl, stir milk and instant coffee granules until coffee is dissolved. Add butter, egg and vanilla. Mix well. Stir into dry mixture. Fold in chocolate chips. Fill greased muffin cups ⅔ full. Bake 17–20 minutes. Serve with Espresso Spread.

Multigrain Muffins

Wesley & Martha Beachy

½ c. all-purpose flour
½ c. cornmeal
½ c. quick oats
¼ c. whole wheat flour
¼ c. brown sugar, packed
3 Tbsp. toasted wheat germ
2 tsp. baking powder

¼ tsp. salt
1 egg, lightly beaten
1 c. milk
¼ c. canola oil
¼ c. chopped nuts
¼ c. raisins

In a bowl, combine first 8 ingredients. In another bowl, mix the egg, milk and canola oil; stir into the dry ingredients, just until moistened. Fold in nuts and raisins. Serve warm. Bake at 375° for 15–18 minutes or until toothpick comes out clean.

French Breakfast Puffs

Cheryl Rose Miller

⅔ c. butter
1 c. sugar
2 eggs
1 tsp. vanilla
1 c. milk

3 c. flour
3 tsp. baking powder
½ tsp. salt
½ tsp. nutmeg

Topping:
6 Tbsp. butter, melted
4 tsp. cinnamon

¼ c. sugar

Cream butter and sugar. Beat in eggs, vanilla and milk. Add dry ingredients. Fill muffin cups or cupcake papers ⅔ full. Bake at 350° for 20–25 minutes. *Topping:* While very warm, dip tops into melted butter or margarine; then roll in a mixture of cinnamon and sugar. Serve warm. Tip: Can also spread on cookie sheet and put sugar and cinnamon mixture on top, then bake.

Corn Mush

Levi & Katie Beachy

6 c. water
2 tsp. salt

2 c. cornmeal
2 c. milk

Cook 45 minutes. Pour into loaf pan to cool. Slice and fry in oil. We think it is delicious with bacon and eggs or with head cheese.

Quick Fried Mush

Orvan & Marilyn Miller

1 c. cornmeal
½ tsp. salt

½ c. hot milk
1 c. hot water

Put cornmeal and salt in a bowl. Add hot milk and water; stir until well mixed. Drop by tablespoonfuls into a hot skillet with oil and fry until crisp. If batter gets too stiff, add a little more hot water.

Ham Gravy

Steve & Lorene Helmuth

1 qt. water
1½ Tbsp. ham base

¼ c. water
¼ c. clear jel

Put 1 quart of water into kettle. Bring to a boil. Stir together ¼ cup of water and ¼ cup clear jel. Once water is boiling add ham base. Stir until dissolved. Keep water to a low boil and slowly pour in clear jel mixture. Return to boiling point. Yield: 8 servings.

Note: Also good using turkey or chicken broth instead of water. And chicken base instead of ham base.

> *The right kind of fear will keep us from doing wrong.*

Tomato Gravy

Orvan & Marilyn Miller

1 c. tomato juice
½ c. water
3 Tbsp. flour
½ tsp. salt

½ c. cream
2 c. milk
2 Tbsp. sugar (optional)

Place juice and water in saucepan and bring to a boil. Meanwhile blend the flour and salt with the cream (I use milk). Add the milk and mix well. Pour into the hot juice, stirring constantly until boiling. May be served with bread, toast, crackers or fried potatoes.

Note: We like to eat it with sunny-side up eggs, and crackers.

Corn Crunch Cereal

Marnita Beachy

2 c. buttermilk or sour milk
1½ c. cornmeal
2 c. flour
1½ c. sugar

1 tsp. salt
1 tsp. soda
1 tsp. baking powder

Mix dry ingredients and add milk. Mix well. Spread into a greased pan. Bake at 350° for 35 minutes. Cool and crumble. Toast dry in 350° oven.

Grape Nuts Cereal

Jeremy Allen Helmuth

4 c. brown sugar, packed
10 c. whole wheat flour
2 tsp. salt
1½ Tbsp. soda

¾ c. margarine
1 Tbsp. vanilla
6 c. buttermilk, soak
    soda in buttermilk

Mix dry ingredients; add the rest. Bake in 2 large cake pans. Eat as cake for breakfast or crumble and bake at 275° for 1½–2 hours, stirring often.

Grape Nuts*

Beachy's Bulk Foods

5 lb. brown sugar
8 lb. (24 c.) whole wheat flour
1¼ Tbsp. salt
2 Tbsp. soda

¾ lb. margarine, melted
1½ tsp. maple flavor
2 Tbsp. vanilla
2½ qt. buttermilk or sour milk

The dough should be fairly thick, if it is too thick (consistency of bread dough) add a little more milk, if too thin (quite sloppy) add more flour. Bake at 350° until done. Then rub through a large screen while still hot. Spread out on cookie sheets and dry at 250° for 1 hour or until crisp. Stir every 15 minutes.

Chocolate Chip Granola Cereal

Alvin & Charlene Kanagy

6 c. quick oatmeal
2 c. brown sugar
2 tsp. salt
4 c. whole wheat flour

1 c. coconut
1½ tsp. soda
1½ c. butter
1 c. chocolate chips

Mix together dry ingredients, except chocolate chips. Add melted butter. Mix well with hands. Place in 2 cake pans and bake at 400° for 30 minutes. Stir often to keep from getting lumpy. Add chocolate chips after cereal is cooled. Very delicious.

Granola

Abner & Sovilla Mae Zook

10 c. quick oats
1¼ c. wheat germ
dash of salt
2½ tsp. cinnamon
5 Tbsp. butter
½ c. brown sugar

¼ c. vegetable oil
½ c. sorghum
½ c. honey
½ tsp. vanilla
½ tsp. maple flavor

Combine oats, wheat germ, salt and cinnamon. Melt together butter and sugar. Add rest of ingredients to butter and sugar mixture, then mix in with the oat mixture. Put in 2 cookie sheets and toast at 275° for 45 minutes or until brown, stirring every 15 minutes.

Granola

Orvan & Marilyn Miller

10 c. quick oats	½ c. vegetable oil
2 c. wheat germ (optional)	½ c. honey
2 c. coconut	2 tsp. vanilla
1½ c. brown sugar	1 tsp. salt
½ c. almonds or sunflower seeds	½ c. raisins

Mix brown sugar and salt into oatmeal. Add rest of ingredients. Bake at 275° for 1 hour, stirring every 15 minutes. When cooled add ½ c. chocolate, butterscotch or any other kind of chips you prefer.

Variations: We like to use homemade pancake syrup instead of honey. You can also use 1 teaspoon vanilla and 1 teaspoon maple flavoring. Is also good with ½ cup peanut butter. If adding peanut butter, reduce heat to 250°.

Golden Krispie Granola*

Beachy's Bulk Foods

24 c. regular oats	2¼ tsp. salt
1 c. wheat germ	1½ c. honey
2 c. wheat bran	1½ c. maple syrup
3 c. pecans	2 c. canola oil
1½ c. unsweetened coconut	6 Tbsp. vanilla
3 c. raw sunflower meats	

Bake at 300° for 1½ hours. Stir every 15 minutes.

Sunrise Granola (Wheat Free) *

Beachy's Bulk Foods

12 c. regular oats
3 c. oat bran
3 c. raw sunflower meats
3 c. sliced almonds
¾ Tbsp. salt

¼ c. vanilla
1½ c. canola oil
1¼ c. honey
1¼ c. maple syrup
1½ c. raisins

Put raisins in ½ hour before done. Bake at 300° for 1½ hours. Stir every 15 minutes.

> When a painting job is done and you close the lid on the can, add plastic wrap between can and cover and close up. No scummy layer on top when reopening.

Appetizers & Beverages

Cheese Ball

Nelson Zook

16 oz. cream cheese
8 oz. Velveeta cheese
1½ tsp. Hickory Smoke flavor
½ tsp. seasoned salt

½ tsp. garlic salt
2 tsp. Worcestershire sauce
2 oz. thin sliced meat

Soften cream cheese and cheese. Chop meat fine. Mix all ingredients together well. Serve chilled with snack crackers.

Cheese Ball

Anna Viola Beachy

16 oz. cream cheese
1 tube Hickory Smoke cheese
2 tsp. onion flakes
½ tsp. garlic salt

2 tsp. Worcestershire sauce
2 tsp. Lawry's seasoning salt
4 oz. chipped ham

Mix all by hand and chill. Form and roll in ½ cup chopped pecans and 2 teaspoon parsley flakes.

Celery Vehicles

Steve & Lorene Helmuth

1 stalk celery
1 Tbsp. peanut butter

8 carrot slices
(4 slices for each vehicle)

Fill celery with peanut butter. Place toothpicks for wheels through sides both in front and back of the celery. Place carrot circle on toothpick for wheels.

Seasoned Pretzels

Willard & Carol Ann Helmuth

1 c. vegetable oil
3 Tbsp. cheddar
   cheese powder

3 Tbsp. sour cream and
   onion powder
1 lb. pretzels

Mix powders and vegetable oil. Pour over pretzels and mix well. Put in large roaster pan and bake at 250° for 30 minutes. Stir often.

Taco Roll-Ups

Melvin & Beth Ann Beachy

1½ lb. ground beef
1 med. onion
1 pkg. taco seasoning

8 oz. shredded cheese
8 oz. cream cheese
1 c. sour cream

Fry ground beef, onion and taco seasoning. Mix together cheese, cream cheese and sour cream. Mix everything together and roll up in flour tortillas. Make approx. 6–8 rolls. Refrigerate then slice and serve with salsa.

Of all the things you wear, your expression is the most important.

Vegetable Crackers

Raymond & Martha Beachy

¼ c. butter, softened or olive oil	2 Tbsp. finely grated carrots
1 c. whole grain flour	dash of red pepper
½ tsp. soda	¼ tsp. salt
¼ tsp. celery salt	½ c. grated cheese
½ tsp. parsley flakes	1–2 Tbsp. cold tomato juice or
1 tsp. finely chopped onions	ketchup

Mix all ingredients except juice until thoroughly combined. Add juice a little at a time. Roll out very thin. Cut. Bake at 350° for 20–25 minutes. Store in a tight container at room temperature.

Finger Jell-O

Jo Anna Sue Miller

3 (3oz.) pkg. or	4 c. boiling water
1¼ c. Jell-O, any flavor	1 c. cold water
4 env. or 4 Tbsp. plain gelatin	

Mix together Jell-O, pour boiling water over Jell-O, stir until dissolved. Add cold water. Pour into a 9"x13" pan. Chill and cut in squares.

Peanut Butter Apple Dip

Orvan & Marilyn Miller

8 oz. cream cheese	1 c. brown sugar
1 c. peanut butter	¼ c. milk

Mix well and serve with apples.

Caramel Dip for Apples

Robert & Dorothy Beachy

½ c. butter
1 can sweetened
  condensed milk

1 c. brown sugar
½ c. corn syrup

Cook for 1 minutes, stirring constantly. Serve warm with apple slices.

Apple Dip

Raymond & Martha Beachy

14 oz. caramels (49 pcs.)
1 can sweetened
  condensed milk

16 oz. cream cheese
1 c. brown sugar
½ tsp. vanilla

Mix caramels and condensed milk with cream cheese, brown sugar and vanilla. Heat all together until melted. Cool.

Cheesy Beef Taco Dip

Marnita Beachy

2 lb. ground beef
1 med. green pepper, chopped
1 lg. onion, finely chopped
1 lb. Velveeta cheese
1 lb. Pepper Jack cheese, cubed
16 oz. taco sauce

10 oz. diced tomatoes and
  green chilies, drained
4 oz. mushrooms, drained
  and chopped
2¼ oz. sliced ripe olives, chopped
tortilla chips

In large skillet, cook beef, onion and pepper. Add cheeses and stir until melted. Add rest of ingredients and mix well. Serve with tortilla chips.

Mexican Dip

Steven & Lorene Helmuth

1 lb. hamburger	1 pkg. taco seasoning
1 jar taco sauce	1 can refried beans
2 c. sour cream	1 pkg. grated cheese

Brown hamburger; add taco seasoning. In a bowl, mix hamburger, taco sauce and refried beans. Spread meat mixture in a 9"x13" pan. Top with sour cream and cheese. Bake at 350° until cheese is melted. Serve with chips.

Note: Pizza sauce can be used instead of taco sauce and less refried beans. Very good!

Pizza Dip

Marnita Beachy

8 oz. cream cheese	⅓ c. finely diced red bell peppers
½ c. pizza sauce	⅓ c. sliced green onions
2 cloves garlic, finely chopped	½ c. shredded mozzarella cheese
½ c. chopped pepperoni	¼ c. shredded fresh basil leaves
2¼ oz. ripe olives, sliced and drained	colored tortilla chips

Set oven control to broil. Mix cream cheese, pizza sauce and garlic. Spread in thin layer on 12" round oven proof plate. Top with pepperoni, olives, peppers and onions. Sprinkle with mozzarella cheese. Broil with top 4" from heat, 1–2 minutes or until cheese is melted. Sprinkle with basil. Serve immediately with chips. Yield: 16 servings.

Fruit Dip

Anna Viola Beachy

8 oz. cream cheese, softened   7 oz. marshmallow creme

Mix until well blended. Dip all kinds of fresh fruit.

Chilled Caramel Mocha Drink

Marnita Beachy

2 c. water   1½ tsp. vanilla
2 c. sugar   ¼ c. Divinci sugar free caramel
½ c. instant coffee   syrup

Bring water to boil and add rest of ingredients. Let this mixture cool. Then chill completely and mix with 1 gal. cold milk. This keeps in refrigerator for quite awhile.

Note: The Divinci caramel syrup can be found in the coffee aisle, you can use regular caramel ice cream syrup, but it doesn't taste as good.

Christmas Punch

Mary Lorene Beachy

12 oz. frozen lemonade   46 oz. pineapple juice
12 oz. frozen orange juice   4 c. water

Mix and freeze. When ready to serve, thaw until slushy; then add 4 quarts 7-Up or Sprite.

Mr. Misty

Mary Lorene Beachy

6 oz. strawberry Jell-O
1½ c. sugar
46 oz. pineapple juice

2 qt. water
7-Up or Sprite

Dissolve Jell-O and sugar in 1 quart boiling water. Add juice and 1 quart cold water. Freeze mixture. Thaw until slushy; then add 7-Up or Sprite to serve. Add what ever amount you like.

Patio Punch

Mary Lorene Beachy

6 oz. frozen orange juice
6 oz. frozen lemonade
1 pkg. cherry Kool-Aid
1 pkg. strawberry Kool-Aid

1 c. sugar
3 qt. water
3 c. pineapple juice

Mix together and refrigerate. When ready to serve, add 1 liter 7-Up and a tray of ice cubes.

Purple Cow

Renita Helmuth

1 c. grape juice, chilled
2–3 Tbsp. sugar (optional)
¼ tsp. vanilla

¼ c. milk
2 lg. scoops vanilla ice cream

Combine grape juice, sugar, vanilla and milk in shaker. Shake well and add ice cream. Shake again until blended. Pour into cold glasses and serve with a smile.

Root Beer

Levi & Katie Beachy

2 c. sugar
½ tsp. yeast

4½ tsp. root beer extract

Put in 1 gallon jar, add lukewarm water to fill. Stir. Leave standing in room temperature for 24 hours. Cool and serve.

Fresh Garden Tea Concentrate

Melvin & Beth Ann Beachy

3 c. fresh tea leaves, packed
4 c. boiling water

1 c. sugar

Heat water to rolling boil; then add tea leaves and continue to boil 1 minute. Then remove from heat and let steep 15 minutes. Remove leaves. Add sugar and cool. Freeze in 1 quart containers. When ready to use, add 3 quarts water to 1 quart concentrate.

Leftover cold tea makes a good fertilizer for houseplants. It acts as an insecticide as well.

Breads & Rolls

Two Hour Buns
(also Bread Sticks)

Melvin & Beth Ann Beachy

2 Tbsp. yeast	2 eggs
2 c. water, divided	1 tsp. salt
½ c. sugar	6 c. flour
½ c. shortening	

Dissolve yeast in 1 cup warm water. Cream sugar and shortening. Heat 1 cup water; add to shortening and sugar. Add eggs and beat well. Add yeast, salt and flour; mix well. Let set 1 hour. Work out, let set another hour and bake at 350° for 10 minutes. Yield: 24 buns.

Bread Sticks: Use Two Hour Bun recipe. Press dough onto a cookie sheet that has been heavily buttered and sprinkled with cornmeal. Rub more soft butter over dough. Sprinkle with Italian seasoning. Cut into strips with pizza cutter. Let rise and bake until golden. Remove from oven and spread more soft butter over top. Sprinkle with Parmesan cheese, and return to oven for a couple of minutes. Serve with spaghetti sauce, pizza sauce or cheese sauce.

60-Minute Hamburger Buns

Willard & Carol Ann Helmuth

2 Tbsp. yeast	3 Tbsp. sugar
¼ c. warm water	¾ tsp. salt
1¼ c. milk	4½ c. flour
¼ c. butter	

Dissolve yeast in warm water, scald milk and cool to lukewarm; then add milk, butter, sugar, salt, and flour to yeast mixture. When dough has been kneaded, cover and set in a warm place for 15 minutes. Roll and cut out for buns and place on a greased cookie sheet, let rise for 15 minutes. Bake at 350° for 15 minutes.

Soft Pretzels

Melvin & Beth Ann Beachy

1½ c. warm water
1 Tbsp. yeast
⅓ c. brown sugar
1 Tbsp. vegetable oil

4–4½ c. flour
¼ c. water and
    2 Tbsp. soda

Cheese Sauce:
2 c. milk
1 tsp. salt

3 Tbsp. flour
cheese

Dissolve yeast in warm water. Add brown sugar and vegetable oil. Add flour. Let rise for ½ hour. Shape into balls about the size of golf balls. Roll out to 10" to 15" long. Shape into pretzels. Dip in soda water. Place on greased cookie sheet. Sprinkle with pretzel salt. Bake at 425° until golden brown on the top. Dip top side of pretzel in melted butter after baked. Dip into your choice of cheese sauce.

Cheese sauce: Stir together milk, salt and flour; boil until thick, stirring constantly. Add cheese of your preferred amount.

Banana Nut Bread *

Beachy's Bulk Foods

Small Batch:	Large Batch:
2 c. sugar	8 c.
1 c. shortening	4 c.
4 eggs	16 eggs
½ c. sour milk or buttermilk	2 c.
4 c. flour	16 c.
2 tsp. soda	8 tsp.
1 tsp. baking powder	4 tsp.
1 tsp. salt	4 tsp.
2 c. bananas	8 c.
1 c. nuts	4 c.

In a large bowl, mix together shortening and sugar. Beat well. Add eggs; beat well. Add milk and bananas, then add dry ingredients. Divide into 2 lb. loaves. Bake at 350° for 40–50 minutes.

Chocolate Chip Carrot Bread

Abner & Sovilla Mae Zook

3 c. flour
1 c. sugar
1 c. brown sugar
2½ tsp. cinnamon
2 tsp. baking powder
1 tsp. soda
1 tsp. salt
1 tsp. ginger

¼ tsp. cloves
3 eggs
¾ c. orange juice
¾ c. vegetable oil
1 tsp. vanilla
2 c. grated carrots
1 c. chocolate chips

In a large bowl, combine the first 9 ingredients. In a small bowl, beat the eggs, orange juice, vegetable oil and vanilla. Stir into the dry ingredients just until moistened. Fold in the carrots and chocolate chips. Put in 2 greased 8"x4"x2" loaf pan. Bake at 350° for 55–60 minutes. Yield: 2 loaves.

Cinnamon Bread

Anna Viola Beachy

white bread dough
brown sugar

cinnamon
maraschino cherries

Take recipe for white bread. When ready to shape into loaves, using rolling pin, roll out dough until 1" thick. Sprinkle with brown sugar and cinnamon. Roll up as tight as possible. Pinch seams and ends together. Take scissors and cut top of bread. (We usually make 5 cuts.) Let rise until doubled in size. Bake at 350° for 30 minutes. Cool. Glaze with icing. Garnish with maraschino cherries.

Sour Cream Cornbread

Orvan & Marilyn Miller

2 c. flour	2 eggs, beaten
2 c. cornmeal	2 c. sour cream
¼ c. sugar	⅔ c. milk
4 tsp. baking powder	4 Tbsp. butter, melted
½ tsp. salt	1 tsp. minced onions (optional)

In a bowl, combine dry ingredients. Add remaining ingredients. Stir just until moistened. Bake in a 9"x13" pan at 400° for 20–25 minutes.

Cornbread

Orvan & Marilyn Miller

1½ c. cornmeal	3 tsp. baking powder
1 c. flour	¼ c. margarine, softened
¼ c. sugar	2 eggs
½ tsp. salt	1½ c. milk

Mix together dry ingredients; add margarine, eggs and milk. Bake in a 9"x13" pan at 350° for at least 30 minutes.

Southern Cornbread

Wesley & Martha Beachy

1 c. self-rising cornmeal	buttermilk or sweet milk
1 egg	(enough to form a cake
pinch of salt	like batter)

Set aside and put 3 tablespoons grease onto griddle and put into oven on 500° until real hot, then mix into batter and put back into the pan and bake until golden brown.

Lemon Bread

Mary Lorene Beachy

1 box lemon cake mix
1 box instant lemon pudding
½ c. vegetable oil

4 eggs
1 c. hot water

Mix all ingredients together for 2 minutes with mixer. Pour into 2 regular or 3 small greased and floured loaf pans. Bake at 350° for 50 minutes.

Friendship Bread*

Beachy's Bulk Foods

1¼ c. milk
1¼ c. flour
1¼ c. sugar
4 c. vegetable oil
2 c. milk
4 c. sugar
12 eggs

4 tsp. vanilla
3 c. vanilla instant pudding
8 c. flour
4 tsp. salt
6 tsp. baking powder
2 tsp. soda
8 tsp. cinnamon

Mix together milk, flour and sugar; let set 4 hours. Then add rest of ingredients. Mix together. Divide into loaves.

Pumpkin Bread *

Beachy's Bulk Foods

Small Batch:	Large Batch:
3 c. sugar	12 c.
1 c. vegetable oil	4 c.
4 eggs	16 eggs
1⅔ c. pumpkin	6 c.
¼ c. water	1 c.
3½ c. flour	14 c.
2 tsp. soda	8 tsp.
2 tsp. salt	8 tsp.
1 tsp. baking powder	4 tsp.
1 tsp. nutmeg	4 tsp.
1 tsp. allspice	4 tsp.
1 tsp. cinnamon	4 tsp.
½ tsp. cloves	2 tsp.

In a large bowl, mix together shortening and sugar. Beat well. Add eggs; beat well. Add pumpkin and water, then add dry ingredients. Divide into 2 lb. loaves. Bake at 350° for 40–50 minutes.

Strawberry Bread

Abner & Sovilla Mae Zook

3 c. flour	10 oz. frozen strawberries,
2 c. sugar	thawed (approx.) 1½ c. fresh
3 tsp. cinnamon	1 tsp. salt
1 tsp. soda	4 eggs, beaten
1 c. chopped pecans	1¼ c. vegetable oil

Mix ingredients. Grease and flour pans. Bake at 325° for 1 hour. Yield: 2 loaves.

Zucchini Bread *

Beachy's Bulk Foods

2 c. sugar	2 tsp. soda
1 c. vegetable oil	½ tsp. baking powder
3 eggs	3 tsp. cinnamon
2 c. grated zucchini	1 tsp. salt
2 tsp. vanilla	1 c. chopped nuts
3 c. flour	

Blend sugar, vegetable oil, eggs, zucchini and vanilla. Sift together flour, soda, baking powder, cinnamon and salt. Add to first mixture, then add nuts. Mix well. Bake at 325° for 1 hour. Yield: 2 loaves.

Note: May use apples instead of zucchini and have apple bread.

Dilly Bread *

Beachy's Bulk Foods
Levi & Katie Beachy

1 pkg. or 1 Tbsp. yeast	2 tsp. dill seed
¼ c. warm water	1 tsp. salt
1 c. cottage cheese	1 egg, unbeaten
2 Tbsp. sugar	¼ tsp. soda
1 Tbsp. minced onions	2¼ c. flour
1 Tbsp. margarine	

Dissolve yeast in warm water. Heat next 6 ingredients to lukewarm. Add egg and soda, mix in flour and yeast. Cover and let rise until double in size. Punch down and shape into loaves. Grease pans well. Let rise again until at least double. Bake at 350° for 40–50 minutes or until golden brown. When it starts browning watch closely, as it browns in a hurry. Brush with margarine and sprinkle with salt.

Double Quick Rolls

Melvin & Beth Ann Beachy

1 Tbsp. yeast	1 egg, beaten
1 c. warm water	2 Tbsp. shortening
2 Tbsp. sugar	1 tsp. salt
2¼ c. flour, divided	

In a bowl, dissolve yeast in water and sugar. Stir in 1 cup flour; beat until smooth. Add egg, shortening and beat in 1¼ cup flour; stir until smooth. Add salt and remaining flour. Scrape sides and cover. Let rise until double about ½ hour. Grease 12 large muffin cups. Punch down raised dough and fill cups ½ full. Let rise in a warm place. Bake at 400° for 15–20 minutes.

Note: Use same as dinner rolls.

Oatmeal Bread *

Beachy's Bulk Foods

2 c. boiling water	2 pkg. or 2 Tbsp. yeast
3 Tbsp. shortening	⅓ c. warm water
⅔ c. brown sugar	5 c. flour
1½ tsp. salt	1 c. oatmeal

Bring first 4 ingredients to a boil. Add oatmeal. Cool until lukewarm, then add yeast that has been dissolved in ⅓ cup water. Add flour and knead well. Let rise until doubled. Form into loaves or dinner rolls. Let rise again and bake at 350° for 30 minutes or until browned nicely. Brush with butter.

Oatmeal Raisin Bread

Anna Viola Beachy

2 c. water
5 Tbsp. yeast
6 c. flour
3¾ c. milk
⅔ c. vegetable oil
5 tsp. salt

⅔ c. sugar
3 eggs
2½ c. quick oats
2½ c. raisins
5 c. flour

Mix together water, yeast, and 6 c. flour. Let set. Then mix together rest of ingredients and add to the first mixture. Mix together then let rise until double. Punch down and let rise again. Divide into 3 loaves. Roll out with rolling pin. Sprinkle with a small amount of water. Enough to make it damp. Then sprinkle with white sugar and cinnamon. Roll together, put in pans, and let rise again. Bake at 350° for 30–35 minutes. When cooled, ice with cinnamon roll icing.

When you take fresh baked bread out of the oven, turn it on its side, so the bottom doesn't get soggy. Bag when still warm, not hot. This makes a soft crust.

Pepper Cheese Bread

Wilmer & Sarah Beachy

1½ Tbsp. salt
¾ c. sugar
¾ c. vegetable oil
3¾ c. warm water
3 Tbsp. yeast

6–7 c. flour
10 eggs, beaten
20 oz. shredded colby cheese
3¾ c. jalapeño peppers, drained
    and chopped

Put salt, sugar, vegetable oil and water into a large bowl, sprinkle yeast on top. Add flour until dough is soft but not sticky. Let rise until double, punch down, let rise again. Beat eggs. Break off small balls of dough, dip into eggs, then put layer into bottom of large bowl. Sprinkle some cheese and peppers over dough. Repeat layers until dough is used up. Line bread pans with waxed paper. Spray paper with cooking spray. Carefully spoon balls of dough into pans until they weigh 1¾ lb. each. Makes 4 or 5 loaves. Let rise about ¾" above pans. Bake at 350° for 40 minutes or until golden brown.

Beachy Family Favorites

Pineapple Braids

Raymond & Martha Beachy

1 c. butter, softened	1 Tbsp. yeast
5 c. flour	¼ c. warm water
½ tsp. salt	¾ c. warm water
3 eggs, beaten	½ c. sugar

Pineapple Filling:

1 can crushed pineapples	6 Tbsp. clear jel
1 c. water	½ c. sugar

Glaze:

1½ c. powdered sugar	3 tsp. melted butter
1–2 Tbsp. hot milk	½ tsp. vanilla

Cut butter into flour and salt in a large mixing bowl with a pastry cutter. Add eggs and yeast that was dissolved in ¼ cup warm water. Add sugar and rest of water. Mix by hand until well mixed. Cover and refrigerate for 5 to 6 hours or overnight. Set dough out until room temperature. Divide dough into 4 parts. Roll each part into a 9"x13" rectangle. Spread ½ cup filling lengthwise down center third of rectangle. Cut 1" wide strips along both sides of filling. Fold strips at an angle across filling alternating from side to side. Cover and let rise until double in size. Bake at 350° for 20–25 minutes. Glaze.

Honey Wheat Bread

Raymond & Martha Beachy

7 c. warm water	¾ c. honey
6¼ oz. cake yeast	8 c. Natural White flour
¾ c. butter	12 c. Bronze Chief flour
2 Tbsp. real salt	

In a large mixing bowl, mix together water, yeast, butter, honey and salt. Stir until dissolved. Add flour and knead until elastic. Cover and let rise, punch down and let rise again. Shape into loaves; let rise. Bake at 350°.

Note: You may need to add more flour if dough is sticky.

Honey Oatmeal Bread

Orvan & Marilyn Miller

2 c. quick oatmeal	1 c. honey
3 c. hot water	2 c. whole wheat flour
2 c. milk, scalded	2–3 Tbsp. yeast
4 Tbsp. vegetable oil	2 eggs, beaten
1 Tbsp. salt	10 c. white flour (approx.)

Soak oatmeal in the hot water for 10 minutes. Then add milk, vegetable oil, salt and honey. Mix and cool to lukewarm. Add whole wheat flour, (I use Golden 86 wheat), yeast and eggs. Mix thoroughly; then add white flour and let rise 1 hour. Punch down and let rise ½ hour. Then form into loaves and place in baking pans. Let rise until double in size. Bake at 350° for 30 minutes.

Wheat Oatmeal Bread

Orvan & Marilyn Miller

1 c. wheat flour	½ c. brown sugar
2 c. quick oats	4 c. boiling water
2 Tbsp. salt	3 Tbsp. yeast
4 Tbsp. butter	10 c. flour (approx.)

Pour boiling water over first 5 ingredients. Cool until lukewarm. Dissolve yeast in 1 cup warm water. Add to batter. Add 3 cups wheat flour and 7 cups white flour or enough to make elastic dough. Set bowl in warm place. Let rise ½ hour. Punch down and let rise again until double in size. Shape into 4 loaves. Let rise again until double in size. Bake at 350° for at least 30 minutes. May also be made into dinner rolls. Brush with margarine when done.

White Bread*

Beachy's Bulk Foods

4 pkg. or 4 Tbsp. yeast	½ c. sugar
1 Tbsp. sugar	1 Tbsp. salt
1 c. water	7 c. lukewarm water
½ c. shortening	22 or 24 c. white flour
(we use peanut oil)	

Mix together shortening, sugar, salt and water with half of flour. Add yeast mixture; then rest of flour. Let rise until double, punch down. Let rise again. Form into 8 loaves. Let rise until at least doubled. Bake at 350° for 30 minutes. Or if you prefer lightly browned bread, bake at 325° for 30 minutes. Turn oven off and let bread set 10 minutes; then remove from oven.

Whole Wheat Bread *

Beachy's Bulk Foods

4 pkg. or 4 Tbsp. yeast
1 Tbsp. sugar
1 c. water
½ c. shortening
½ c. sugar or honey (we use sugar)

1 Tbsp. salt
7 c. lukewarm water
8 c. whole wheat flour
14–16 c. white flour

Mix together first 3 ingredients; let set. Mix together shortening, sugar, salt and water with wheat flour and 2 cup white flour. Add yeast mixture; then rest of flour. Let rise until double. Form into 8 loaves. Let rise until at least doubled. Bake at 350° for 30 minutes.

Pizza Hut Bread Sticks

Lamar Jay Miller

1½ c. warm water
1 Tbsp. yeast
1 Tbsp. sugar

1¼ tsp. salt
3 Tbsp. vegetable oil
4 c. flour

Butter Mixture:
¾ c. melted butter
3 Tbsp. Parmesan cheese
1 Tbsp. Italian seasoning

1 tsp. garlic powder
1 Tbsp. dried parsley

Mix dough. Let rise until double in size. Roll out in large squares and cut in strips 5" long. Dip in butter mixture. Twist and place on sheet. Bake at 375° for 10 minutes or until light browned. Serve with warm pizza, cheese sauce or soup.

Butter Dips

Melvin & Beth Ann Beachy

⅓ c. butter

2¼ c. flour

3½ tsp. baking powder

1 c. milk

1 Tbsp. sugar

1½ tsp. salt

Melt butter in a 9"x13" pan. Mix together rest of ingredients. Roll out on floured surface ¾–1" thick. Cut in strips 1" wide and about 5" long. Roll in the melted butter and lay strips side by side in pan. Bake at 450° for 15–20 minutes. For a different flavor sprinkle with garlic salt before baking. Very good with jelly or eat like bread sticks.

Butterhorns

Willard & Carol Ann Helmuth

1 c. milk

¼ c. sugar

1 Tbsp. yeast

2 eggs, beaten

¾ c. real butter

½ tsp. salt

¼ c. warm water

4 c. flour

Heat milk only until you can stand your finger in it. Then add butter, sugar and salt and mix until butter is melted. Add yeast mixture: ¼ cup warm water and 1 tablespoon yeast, let set until foamy. Stir, then add eggs and flour. Let rise until double about 1½ hour. Work down. Divide dough in 2 portions and roll out each portion ¼" thick in a 12" circle, cut like a pie and roll up and bake at 350° until very light brown. Frost and enjoy.

Caramel Pecan Rolls*

Beachy's Bulk Foods

4 Tbsp. margarine   1 Tbsp. water
½ c. brown sugar   ½ c. pecans

Melt margarine, brown sugar and water. Bring almost to boiling, remove from heat and add pecans. Pour into roll pan. When cooled, take cinnamon roll dough, and drop on top of caramel filling. Let rise and bake at 350° for at least 20 minutes. When removed from oven, while still hot, turn upside down onto a plate. Let set a few moments then remove pan and scrape caramel filling onto rolls.

Cream Sticks

Lavern Helmuth

2 pkg. dry yeast
1 c. warm water
½ c. margarine
⅔ c. sugar
2 eggs, well beaten

½ tsp. salt
1 c. milk, scalded
1 tsp. vanilla
6 c. flour

Cream Stick Filling:
2⅓ c. powdered sugar
¼ tsp. salt
1 egg white, beaten
2 Tbsp. water

1 c. white sugar
1 tsp. vanilla
½ c. Crisco

Frosting:
½ c. brown sugar
4 Tbsp. butter

2 Tbsp. milk
1 tsp. vanilla

Soak yeast in warm water. Put margarine, sugar, eggs and salt into scalded milk. Let cool; then add to the yeast. Add vanilla and flour. Let rise once. Roll out and form into 1½"x3½" sticks. Let rise again. Deep fat fry. Make a slit in the side and fill with cream stick filling. *Cream Stick Filling:* Mix together powdered sugar, salt and egg white and set aside. Mix together water and white sugar; boil 1 minute. Add to first mixture. Cream in vanilla and Crisco. Frost with recipe included, if desired. *Frosting:* Mix and heat to a boil. Cool. Add powdered sugar and vanilla.

Note: Boiled frosting will not harden if vanilla is added while cooking.

Church Cakes

Levi & Katie Beachy

7 c. milk
7 c. sugar
1½ c. lard

pinch of salt
18 c. flour

Heat first 4 ingredients to lukewarm. Mix 5 heaping tablespoons flour in hot water to make a paste. Add 3 tablespoons yeast which has been put in a little warm water and a little sugar. Let set until light; add to milk mixture which has been heated; then pour into flour. Let rise until double; work out in 2" balls. Let rise until double; bake at 350°. When they come out of oven brush with sweet cream.

Cinnamon Rolls*

Beachy's Bulk Foods

3 c. hot water
¾ c. donut mix
1 c. warm water
4 pkg. or 4 Tbsp. yeast
1 c. peanut oil

1 c. sugar
4 tsp. salt
4 eggs
15 c. flour

Mix hot water and instant potato flakes. Mix together warm water and yeast and let set. Mix together potatoes, sugar, salt and peanut oil; add 7 cups flour. Beat eggs and add along with yeast, add the rest of the flour. Let rise until double. Roll out on lightly floured surface. Spread with melted margarine. Sprinkle with brown sugar and cinnamon. Roll together fairly tight. Cut in approximately ¾" slices. Set rolls in greased pan. Let rise until doubled. Bake at 350° for 20–25 minutes or until golden brown.

Cinnamon Roll

Darren Zook

1⅓ c. butter
2 c. milk, scalded
3 Tbsp. yeast
2 c. lukewarm water
1 c. fructose

2 c. mashed potatoes
4 tsp. salt
4 eggs, beaten
14–15 c. flour

Melt butter in scalded milk. Dissolve yeast in lukewarm water. In large bowl, mix fructose, mashed potatoes and salt. Add milk and butter. Stir in 6 cups flour. Add beaten eggs; stir well. Add yeast mixture; stir well. Add rest of the flour. Let rise until double. Roll out and spread with melted butter. It takes about ½ cup butter to do this batch. Sprinkle with brown sugar and cinnamon; roll together and cut. Put in pans and let rise. Bake at 350° until nice and brown. Ice with your favorite icing.

Cinnamon Roll Icing*

Beachy's Bulk Foods

3 c. powdered sugar
1 Tbsp. perma-flo

½ tsp. vanilla
¾ c. milk

Mix well and spread. May use more or less milk, just add until you have the consistency you want.

Cinnamon Filling for Tea Ring

Melvin & Beth Ann Beachy

1 Tbsp. butter
3 Tbsp. perma-flo
1 c. water

½ c. sugar
1 tsp. cinnamon

Mix everything together and cook until boiling; boil for 1 minute.

Fruit Filled Rolls

Levi & Katie Beachy

Take cinnamon roll dough and roll out on countertop. Instead of adding margarine, brown sugar and cinnamon, spread on any pie filling of your choice. Make only a thin layer. Roll up and cut. Put in pans and let rise. Bake at 350° for 20 minutes. Glaze when cooled.

Cinna-Swirls

Verna Kay Zook

1½ c. milk
2 Tbsp. yeast
¾ c. warm water
¼ c. fructose
2 tsp. salt

½ c. vegetable oil
2 eggs, beaten
1 c. donut mix
4–5 c. flour

Topping:
1 c. sugar

2 tsp. cinnamon

Glaze:
2 lb. powdered sugar
1 Tbsp. perma-flo

⅞ c. water

Heat milk to scalding. Dissolve yeast in warm water. In large mixing bowl, combine fructose, salt, vegetable oil and milk. Put in ½ of flour; mix well. Add beaten eggs; mix well. Add yeast mixture; mix well. Add donut mix and rest of flour. Let rise 1 hour. Roll out and sprinkle with cinnamon and sugar mixture. Roll up dough as jelly roll. Cut in ¾" slices. Let rise ½ hour. Deep fat fry. Glaze Cinn-Swirls while hot.

Doughnuts

Levi & Katie Beachy

1 qt. milk
1 c. shortening
1 c. sugar
2 Tbsp. salt

1 c. mashed potatoes
6 egg yolks
3 pkg. or 3 Tbsp. dry yeast
13 c. flour

Heat milk to almost boiling, put shortening, sugar, salt and potatoes in milk. Beat egg yolks and add along with yeast. Add flour. Let rise about 1 hour. Roll out and cut. Let rise until double in size. Deep fat fry in 400° oil. Glaze.

Doughnuts

Melvin & Beth Ann Beachy

4 c. warm water   4 lb. Dawn donut mix
4 Tbsp. yeast

Glaze:
3 lb. powdered sugar   2 Tbsp. butter
2 Tbsp. cornstarch   hot water

Mix water and yeast together, let set until foamy; then add to donut mix and work well. Let rise until double in size. Work out on floured surface and roll out about ¾" thick and cut; let rise a little; then fry in 375° oil. Dip in glaze and put on cooling racks to drip or hang on a dowel rod.

When the yeast mixture, (yeast and water) foams and bubbles in 10 minutes you know the yeast is still active.

Salad, Soup, & Sandwiches

Broccoli Cauliflower Salad

Anna Viola Beachy

1 bunch broccoli
1 bunch cauliflower
1 sm. onion

2 c. grated cheese
6 pcs. fried bacon

Sauce:
1 c. sour cream
1 c. salad dressing

½ c. sugar
½ tsp. salt

Cut up broccoli, cauliflower and onion. Mix with cheese and bacon. Mix sauce and pour over all.

Broccoli Ramen Salad

Marnita Beachy

broccoli florets
curly leaf or Romaine lettuce
chopped green onions
½ c. butter

4 c. chopped pecans
3 pkg. chicken flavored Ramen
  noodles, crushed

Dressing:
2 c. sugar
2 c. vegetable oil
⅔ c. red wine vinegar

1 Tbsp. soy sauce
3 pkg. seasoning mix from
  Ramen noodles

Fill a Tupperware fix-n-mix bowl ½ full of broccoli florets; next fill up bowl with curly leaf or Romaine lettuce, chopped. Add some chopped onions. Toast 4 cups pecan pieces in ¼ cup butter over low heat until golden. Toast 3 pkg. of crushed Ramen noodles in ¼ cup butter, stirring occasionally. Cool. *Dressing:* Beat together with wire whisk. Before serving add dressing and toss well. You may not need all the dressing.

We found this cook-
book at the little
store in Luther
where we get our
popcorn. It is
Amish.

Enjoy!

Cranberry Salad

Raymond & Martha Beachy

8 oz. cream cheese
1 c. sugar
2 c. sour cream
2 cans cranberry sauce

16 oz. Cool Whip
1 can crushed pineapples
nuts, if desired

Mix together cream cheese and sugar. Add sour cream and cranberry sauce. Fold in Cool Whip, pineapples and nuts. Freeze.

Cucumber Salad

Abner & Sovilla Mae Zook

6 c. thinly sliced cucumbers
2 c. thinly sliced onions
1 c. salad dressing
1 c. sour cream

½ c. sugar
1 tsp. salt
2 Tbsp. lemon juice

Mix all ingredients in bowl, except cucumbers and onions. Let set for 5 minutes until sugar melts; then stir again. Pour over cucumbers and onions. Delicious!

Fresh lemon juice will remove onion scent from hands.

Lettuce Haystack

LaWayne Ray Helmuth

Ritz crackers, crushed
chopped lettuce
cooked rice
fried meat
diced tomatoes

chopped celery
shredded carrots
chopped onions
cheese sauce

Make a "Haystack" by stacking each ingredient in order given. Top with cheese sauce. Delicious!

Note: May also use corn chips or any kind of chips.

Lime Cottage Cheese Salad

Renita Faye Helmuth

1 sm. pkg. lime Jell-O
½ c. boiling water
2 c. mini marshmallows

1 c. drained pineapples
2 c. whipped topping
1 c. sm. curd cottage cheese

Dissolve Jell-O in boiling water; add marshmallows to melt. Stir in pineapples. Chill until slightly thickened. Fold in cottage cheese and whipped cream.

Potato Salad (large batch)

Wilmer & Sarah Beachy

36 c. potatoes, cooked and
   shredded
6 doz. hard-boiled eggs

12 c. finely chopped celery
6 c. chopped onions

Dressing:

18 c. salad dressing
1 c. + 2 Tbsp. vinegar
1 c. + 2 Tbsp. mustard

½ c. salt
9 c. sugar
4 c. milk

Mix all dressing ingredients and add to potatoes, eggs, celery, and onions; mix well. Yield: 6 gallons.

Note: Best when mixed a couple days ahead.

Potato Salad (small batch)

Wilmer & Sarah Beachy

12 c. potatoes, cooked
   and shredded
12 eggs, hard-boiled

2 c. chopped celery
1 c. chopped onions

Dressing:

3 c. salad dressing
3 Tbsp. vinegar
3 Tbsp. mustard

4 tsp. salt
1½ c. sugar
½ c. milk

Mix all dressing ingredients and add to potatoes, eggs, celery and onions and mix well. Yield: 1 gallon.

Note: Best when mixed a couple days ahead.

Potato Salad

Melvin & Beth Ann Beachy

12 c. potatoes, cooked and shredded	12 eggs, hard-boiled and sliced
	1½ c. chopped celery

Dressing:

3 c. Miracle Whip	¼ c. vinegar
2½ c. sugar	3 Tbsp. mustard
½ c. milk	3 tsp. salt

Cook potatoes. Cool and shred. Slice eggs and chop celery. Mix dressing ingredients and pour over potatoes, eggs and celery. Mix together. Refrigerate several hours before serving. Yield: 1 gallon.

Potato Salad

Levi & Katie Beachy

30 lb. potatoes, cooked and put through salsa master	20 stalks celery, diced
	30 hard-boiled eggs

Dressing:

15–20 c. salad dressing	2 Tbsp. mustard
3 cans Milnot	salt to taste
4 c. sugar	

Milk may be used instead of Milnot. If Milnot is used it may be kept in refrigerator for a week.

Tossed Taco Salad

Omer & Dorothy Beachy

1 head lettuce, chopped
1 bunch green onions,
   chopped (optional)
4 tomatoes, chunked
1 (5½ oz.) pkg. taco chips

1 lb. ground beef
8 oz. Thousand Island dressing
1 can red kidney beans, drained
12 oz. cheese, grated

Mix everything together except beef and dressing. Brown ground beef and drain, add to the salad. Add dressing and toss well. Serve.

Vegetable Pizza

Melvin & Beth Ann Beachy

2 pkg. crescent rolls
8 oz. cream cheese
16 oz. sour cream
1 pkg. Hidden Valley Ranch
   dressing mix

lettuce
vegetable, any kind
shredded cheese

Roll out crescent rolls on cookie sheet and bake at 350° until light brown. Cool. Mix cream cheese, sour cream and dressing mix and spread over cooled crust. Add lettuce and any kind of chopped up vegetables; then top with shredded cheese.

Vegetable Pizza

Anna Viola Beachy

Part 1:
2 pkg. buttermilk biscuits

Part 2:
16 oz. sour cream

1 pkg. Hidden Valley
Ranch dressing mix

Part 3:
chopped vegetables of
   your choice
eggs

ham
shredded cheese

    Part 1: Press biscuits thinly onto a cookie sheet. Bake and cool. I use the Melt in your Mouth Biscuits recipe. *Part 2:* Mix sour cream and Hidden Valley mix and spread on cooled crust. *Part 3:* Layer with lettuce, shredded carrots, chopped celery, cauliflower, chopped ham, shredded eggs, tomatoes and shredded cheese. Use your imagination! Anything you like in a salad is also good on this pizza.

Dressing

Treva Kay Beachy

2 c. salad dressing
1 c. sugar
salt and pepper

dash of vinegar
milk

    Mix all ingredients very well. Store in a jar in the refrigerator. Great for lettuce salads.

French Dressing

Abner & Sovilla Mae Zook

2 Tbsp. onion	¼ c. vinegar
¾ c. sugar	1 tsp. salt
⅓ c. ketchup	1 Tbsp. lemon juice
½ c. vegetable oil	1 Tbsp. salad dressing

Put in blender and mix.

Note: Our favorite dressing to put on taco salad.

Miracle Whip Salad Dressing

Levi & Katie Beachy

Part 1:

1 c. water	½ c. vinegar
⅔ c. flour	

Part 2:

1 egg + water to make ¾ c.	2 tsp. salt
¾ c. butter	½ tsp. dry mustard
⅔ c. sugar	1 tsp. ReaLemon juice

Part 1: Blend together. Cook and set aside. *Part 2:* Mix together and beat real well. Drop first part into second part a spoonful at a time, and beat very, very well, after each addition.

Ranch Dressing

Raymond & Martha Beachy

1 c. mayonnaise
1 c. sour cream
½ c. buttermilk
¼ c. vegetable oil
1 Tbsp. parsley

⅛ tsp. garlic powder
⅛ tsp. paprika
1 Tbsp. onion flakes
1 tsp. Lawry's seasoned salt
½ tsp. salt

Mix all together and refrigerate. May need to add milk to thin to right consistency.

Super Salad Dressing

Melvin & Beth Ann Beachy

1 c. mayonnaise
¼ c. sugar
¼ c. water

1 tsp. vinegar
2 Tbsp. Salad Seasoning Supreme

Mix all together until smooth and creamy with wire whip. This is yummy on taco salad or burritos.

Sweet and Sour Dressing

Steven & Lorene Helmuth

4 c. salad dressing
2 c. sugar
1 c. vegetable oil
¼ c. vinegar

½ c. mustard
dash of celery seed
1 tsp. salt

Mix well and refrigerate. Don't mix in a blender.

Tossed Salad Dressing

Melvin & Beth Ann Beachy

2 c. mayonnaise
1 Tbsp. mustard
¼ tsp. celery salt
½ tsp. onion salt

¼ c. vinegar
¼ c. vegetable oil
¾ c. sugar

Blend or beat very well.

Cream of Broccoli Soup

Abner & Sovilla Mae Zook

3 c. diced potatoes
1 lb. broccoli
½ c. chopped onions
2 cans milk

3 cans cream of broccoli soup
2 cans evaporated milk
½ lb. Velveeta cheese

Cook potatoes, broccoli and onions in salted water. Don't drain off water. Add remaining ingredients and heat. Do not boil! Yield: 1 gallon.

Note: You can add 1 lb. meat of your choice.

Cauliflower Soup

Abner & Sovilla Mae Zook

1 head cauliflower
1 qt. green beans with juice
1 pt. canned hamburger or
   1 lb. hamburger, browned

½ c. chopped onions
cheese

Cook cauliflower and onions until barely soft. Add green beans and hamburger. Thicken with ½ cup flour and 1 cup milk. Add cheese last.

Cheddar Potato Chowder

Wesley & Martha Beachy

2 c. water
2 c. diced red potatoes
1 c. diced carrots
½ c. diced celery
¼ c. chopped onions
1 tsp. salt
¼ tsp. pepper
¼ c. all-purpose flour
2 c. milk
2 c. (8 oz.) shredded cheese
1 c. cubed, fully cooked ham

In a Dutch oven, combine first 7 ingredients. Bring to a boil. Reduce heat; cover and simmer for 10–12 minutes or until tender. Meanwhile place flour in a large saucepan, gradually whisk in milk. Bring to boil over medium heat; cook. Stir for 20 minutes or until thickened. Remove from heat. Add cheese; stir until melted. Stir the ham and cheese sauce into undrained veggies. Yield: 7 servings.

Cheeseburger Soup

Steve & Lorene Helmuth

½ lb. hamburger
¾ c. chopped onions
¾ c. carrots
¾ c. celery
1 tsp. parsley flakes
¾ tsp. salt
¼ tsp. pepper
4 Tbsp. butter
3 c. chicken broth
4 c. diced potatoes
¼ c. flour
1 c. shredded cheese
1½ c. milk

Brown beef, sauté onions, carrots, celery and parsley with 1 tablespoon butter for 10 minutes. Add broth, potatoes and beef. Simmer for 10–12 minutes. Melt rest of butter; add flour and cook for 4 minutes. Add to soup. Add milk and cheese when ready to serve.

Chicken Chowder Soup

Orvan & Marilyn Miller

3 c. deboned chicken
4 c. chicken broth
1 Tbsp. celery salt or
   2 c. diced celery
2 c. diced potatoes
2 c. diced carrots

¼ c. butter or margarine
1 tsp. salt
¾ c. flour mixed with
   4 c. milk
2 c. Velveeta cheese

Mix first 7 ingredients and bring to a boil. Slowly add flour mixed with milk and bring to a boil. Add cheese. Serves 20.

Chicken Noodle Soup to Can

Orvan & Marilyn Miller

meat from 4 chickens or
   however much you desire
1 gal. cooked noodles
salt to taste
chicken seasoning to taste

1 c. chopped onions
½ gal. chopped celery
½ gal. chopped carrots
½ gal. chopped potatoes

Cook each vegetable separately until nearly done. Cold pack 2 hours. (I like to use homemade noodles.) Heat to boiling.

Note: This is very good when you open a can and add several slices cheese.

Chili Soup

Raymond & Martha Beachy

4 lb. hamburger
1 can chili beans
2 c. stewed tomatoes
1 qt. tomato juice
1 Tbsp. parsley flakes

1 Tbsp. Italian seasoning
2–3 Tbsp. chili powder
6 Tbsp. cornstarch or perma-flo
salt to taste

Fry and chop hamburger in a 6 quart kettle. Drain off excess fat. Add rest of ingredients except cornstarch. Add water to kettle until about 1" from top. Let simmer 5–10 minutes. Mix cornstarch (or perma-flo) with water until it pours easily. Stir into soup and bring to a boil again. Use more cornstarch if you like a thicker soup.

Chilly Day Soup

Renita Faye Helmuth

1 lg. carrot
3 sm. onions
1 qt. potatoes, peeled and sliced
2 Tbsp. rice (optional)

2 Tbsp. macaronies (optional)
1 tsp. salt
2 c. milk
1 tsp. butter

Chop carrots and potatoes; boil until soft. Add all the other ingredients and serve.

Note: Water with ½ milk may be used too.

Country Potato Soup

Landon Zook

6 c. diced potatoes	2 c. sour cream
1 c. carrots	3 c. milk
1 c. onions	6 Tbsp. flour
6 c. water	2 Tbsp. parsley flakes
2 Tbsp. chicken base	1 lb. ham, cubed
1½–2 tsp. salt	Velveeta cheese
½ tsp. pepper	

Cook potatoes, carrots, onions, water, chicken base, salt and pepper in an 8 quart kettle until vegetables are tender. Blend together sour cream, milk and flour; gradually add to soup mixture. Cook over low heat, stirring constantly until thickened. Add parsley flakes, ham and some Velveeta cheese. Add more milk if you want it thinner.

Tomato Vegetable Soup to Can

Steve & Lorene Helmuth

3 lb. hamburger	6 tsp. chili powder
4 med. onions	4 tsp. salt
2 qt. diced potatoes	1 tsp. pepper
1 qt. diced carrots	1½ c. brown sugar
3 c. diced celery	2 c. ketchup
2 (15.5 oz.) cans chili beans	2½ gal. tomato juice

Fry hamburger with onions. Cook potatoes and carrots, do not drain. Mix everything together in 20 quart stockpot and bring to boil; add 3 cups perma-flo (make paste with water). Bring back to a boil. Cold pack 3 hours. Yield: 17–18 quarts.

Fried Onions

Levi & Katie Beachy

Melt ½ cup margarine in pan. Slice onions into melted margarine. Stir, making onion rings. Turn burner on medium-low and fry until soft, stirring occasionally.

Sloppy Joe

Alvin & Charlene Kanagy

1 lb. hamburger	¾ c. water
¼ c. quick oats	¾ c. ketchup
chopped onions (optional)	½ tsp. Worcestershire sauce
1 tsp. salt	1½ Tbsp. mustard
⅛ tsp. pepper	¼ c. brown sugar
2–3 Tbsp. flour	

Mix hamburger, quick oats, onions, salt and pepper; brown. Sprinkle with flour and stir. Add water and simmer. Add ketchup, Worcestershire sauce, mustard and brown sugar, simmer until heated through. Serve on bread or buns. Delicious with cheese and pickles.

Sloppy Joe

Orvan & Marilyn Miller

2 lb. ground beef	¾ c. milk
¼ tsp. pepper	2 tsp. salt
1½ tsp. salt	½ c. ketchup
3 Tbsp. minced onions	3 Tbsp. brown sugar
¾ c. quick oats	1 Tbsp. mustard

Brown first 4 ingredients in skillet; then add quick oats and milk. Cook just a little. Add salt, ketchup, brown sugar and mustard. Simmer for 10–15 minutes longer, stirring once or twice.

Subwheel For 12

Edward Beachy

½ c. rolled oats
½ c. boiling water
2 Tbsp. butter
16 oz. pkg. Hot Roll Mix

¾ c. warm water
2 eggs, beaten
1 Tbsp. dried, chopped onions

Combine oats, boiling water and butter; let set 5 minutes. Dissolve yeast from Roll Mix in warm water; add to oats mixture with eggs and onions. Add flour from mix, stir well. Do not knead. Press dough in a 10" circle on greased pizza pan. Let rise until double. Bake at 350° for 25–30 minutes. Cool, split lengthwise. Combine ½ cup mayonnaise and 4 teaspoon mustard. Spread over cut sides of loaf. Layer with lettuce leaves, 8 oz. thinly sliced ham and 8 oz. turkey breast, 8 oz. sliced cheese, 2 large sliced tomatoes, 1 green pepper, sliced thin and 1 medium onion sliced thin. Cut into wedges.

Grilled Hamburgers

Melvin & Beth Ann Beachy

1 lb. hamburger
1 egg
2 slices onion, chopped fine
8 sm. crackers, crushed

½ tsp. salt
⅓ tsp. pepper
2 Tbsp. milk
1 tsp. Worcestershire sauce

Mix well; form patties and grill.

Pizza Burgers

Orvan & Marilyn Miller

2 lb. hamburger or sausage
2 tsp. salt
⅛ tsp. pepper

1 can cream of mushroom soup
1 pt. pizza sauce
onions and peppers to taste

Fry meat and add rest of ingredients. Butter slices of bread, spoon meat mixture onto bread, add a slice of cheese to each piece of bread. Bake at 400° for 5–10 minutes until cheese is melted.

Soft Pretzels Sandwiches

Merlyn Helmuth

1¼ c. warm water
¼ c. brown sugar
1 Tbsp. yeast
1 tsp. vanilla

1 tsp. salt
2 c. all-purpose flour
2 c. bread flour

Mix all ingredients together. Roll out dough as thin as possible with a rolling pin. Cut in 5"x7" pieces. Place a hot dog, a slice of cheese and a small amount of ketchup on each piece. Roll together and press edges tightly. Bake at 350° for 20 minutes or until nice and brown. These can be enjoyed immediately or frozen for later use.

Ham and Cheese Sticky Buns

Alvin & Charlene Kanagy

1 pkg. whole wheat dinner rolls   1 lb. Swiss cheese
½ lb. ham, sliced

Sauce:
½ c. butter   2 Tbsp. mustard
2 Tbsp. poppy seeds   2 Tbsp. Worcestershire sauce
⅓ c. brown sugar

Heat sauce and boil 2 minutes. Take all of the dinner rolls and cut the whole layer in half, without separating the individual buns, place the bottom half of the buns in a 9"x13" greased pan. Layer ham and cheese and replace the top layer of buns. Pour heated sauce on top. Bake uncovered for 10 minutes; then cover with tin foil and bake 10 more minutes at 350°. Serves 12. Delicious!

Your African Violets will bloom longer and more abundantly if you stick a few rusty nails in the soil alongside them.

Meats & Main Dishes

Corn Dogs

1 lb. hot dogs	1 Tbsp. sugar
1½ c. all-purpose flour	¾ tsp. salt
1½ tsp. baking powder	⅓ c. cornmeal
1½ tsp. dry mustard	1⅓ c. milk
1 egg	½ c. all-purpose flour
1 Tbsp. vegetable oil	

This is to roll hot dogs in. Heat hot dogs before frying, use shortening for deep fat frying.

Chicken Strips

Melvin & Beth Ann Beachy

chicken breasts, cut in strips

Marinate in Italian dressing for 24 hours. Also good if you don't have time to marinate. Dip in butter, roll in crushed cracker crumbs (something buttery like Club or Townhouse crackers). Lay on sprayed or lightly greased cookie sheet. Sprinkle with garlic powder and sesame seeds. Bake at 350°–375° for 30–45 minutes, until golden brown. For making cracker crumbs crush them very fine.

Barbecue Chicken

Steven James Helmuth

1 c. vinegar
1½ c. water
½ c. butter or margarine
2 Tbsp. Worcestershire sauce

½ tsp. onion salt
¼ tsp. garlic salt
3 tsp. salt
pinch of pepper

Place all ingredients in a saucepan and bring to a boil. Soak chicken in this sauce for 1–2 hours. Now it is ready to grill. Dip while grilling. Can also place chicken in shallow pan to finish.

Chicken Coating

Melvin & Beth Ann Beachy

4 c. flour
¼ c. salt
3 Tbsp. paprika
2 tsp. garlic powder

2 tsp. onion powder
4 c. very fine cracker crumbs
2 Tbsp. sugar

Mix well to distribute all ingredients evenly. Store in container to use once needed. Dip chicken into a mixture of 1 egg and ⅓ cup milk beaten well. Then dip into coating and bake at 350° for 1 hour.

Honey Mustard Dressing

Melvin & Beth Ann Beachy

1¾ c. honey
1½ c. brown sugar

3 c. mayonnaise
1 c. mustard

Mix all ingredients with wire whip. This is really good on grilled chicken breasts.

Brine for Grilled Chicken

Alvin & Charlene Kanagy

2 c. vinegar
2 c. water
1 c. butter
½ c. salt

5 Tbsp. Worcestershire sauce
½ tsp. garlic salt
½ tsp. pepper
6 chicken halves

Mix together all ingredients except chicken and heat to boiling. Cool, then pour over chicken halves. Soak 24 hours, then barbecue. No need to baste while barbecuing when presoaking with this.

Barbecued Meatballs

Mary Lorene Beachy, Abner & Sovilla Mae Zook

3 lb. ground beef
12 oz. evaporated milk
1 c. oatmeal
1 c. cracker crumbs
2 eggs

½ c. chopped onions
½ tsp. garlic powder
2 tsp. salt
½ tsp. pepper
2 tsp. chili powder

Sauce:
2 c. ketchup
½–1 c. brown sugar
½ tsp. Liquid Smoke

½ tsp. garlic powder
¼ c. chopped onions

Meatballs: Combine all ingredients (mixture will be soft) and shape into walnut size balls. Place meatballs in a single layer on wax paper-lined cookie sheet. Freeze until solid. Store frozen meatballs in freezer bags. Place frozen meatballs in a 9"x13" baking pan. Pour sauce over the meatballs. Bake at 350° for 1 hour. Yield: 80 meatballs.

Note: Meatballs don't have to be frozen before baking. Thirty minutes baking time is about right if not frozen. Meatballs do not need to be fried.

Delicious Barbecued Meatballs

Renita Faye Helmuth

6 c. hamburger
1 c. milk
2 c. oatmeal
2 eggs
½ c. chopped onions

2 tsp. salt
½ tsp. pepper
¾ tsp. chili powder
½ tsp. garlic salt (optional)

Sauce:
2 c. ketchup
1 c. brown sugar

2 tsp. Hickory Smoke

Mix all ingredients. Place in 9"x13" pan. Pour sauce over mixture and bake at 350° for 1 hour.

Prize Winning Meatloaf

Wilmer & Sarah Beachy

1½ lb. ground beef
1 c. tomato juice
¾ c. quick oats
¼ c. chopped onions

1½ tsp. salt
¼ tsp. pepper
1 egg, beaten

Combine all ingredients; mix well. Press firmly in an ungreased pan. Bake at 350° for about 1 hour. Let set 5 minutes before slicing.

Mock Hamloaf

Steve & Lorene Helmuth

1 lb. hamburger
½ lb. hot dogs, ground

1 c. cracker crumbs
1 egg

Syrup:
¾ c. brown sugar
¾ c. water
1 Tbsp. vinegar

½ tsp. mustard
salt and pepper

Mix meat with cracker crumbs, egg and half of the syrup. Shape into loaf. Pour rest of syrup over loaf. Bake at 325° for 1½ hour.

Poor Man's Steak

Orvan & Marilyn Miller

2 lb. ground beef
2 c. cracker crumbs
2 c. milk

2 eggs
2 Tbsp. minced onions
salt and pepper to taste

Mix and press into a large flat pan. (Cookie sheets work real well.) Let set overnight. Cut in squares, roll in flour. Fry in a skillet with oil until brown. Put in a casserole dish with a slice of cheese on each piece of meat.

Note: (Optional) Mix 1 can cream of mushroom soup with 1 can milk; pour over all. Bake at 350° for 1 hour.

Swedish Meatballs

Orvan & Marilyn Miller

1 lb. ground beef	1½ tsp. salt
½ lb. ground pork	⅛ tsp. pepper
½ c. minced onions	1 tsp. Worcestershire sauce
(only about 1 tsp. boughten)	1 egg
¾ c. fine cracker crumbs	½ c. milk

Meatball Gravy:

¼ c. flour	⅛ tsp. pepper
1 tsp. paprika	2 c. boiling water
½ tsp. salt	¾ c. cream

Mix all ingredients together thoroughly. Shape into balls the size of a walnut. Brown in ¼ cup of hot fat or vegetable oil. Remove meatballs and make gravy. Return meatballs to gravy and cook 15–20 minutes. This is also delicious shaped into patties and fried like hamburgers. *Meatball Gravy:* Stir flour, paprika, salt and pepper into hot fat in skillet. Stir in boiling water and cream.

Roaster Full Chicken Casserole

Wilmer & Sarah Beachy

3–5 cut-up chicken breasts	6 qt. mashed potatoes
3 cans cream of chicken soup	8 oz. cream cheese
Lawry's seasoning salt	16 oz. sour cream
Greek seasoning	Velveeta cheese

Fill bottom of a large roaster with chicken breasts. Season with Lawry's salt and Greek seasoning. Pour cream of chicken soup on top. Bake at 350° for 1 hour. Cook potatoes and mash them, add cream cheese & sour cream. Put on top of meat. Top with cheese and bake until cheese is melted.

Hungarian Chicken with Potatoes

Melvin & Beth Ann Beachy

2 c. cubed, cooked chicken
2 c. macaroni, cooked
   and drained
½ lb. Velveeta cheese
1 can cream of mushroom

2 c. cooked potatoes, cubed
2 c. chicken broth
bread crumbs
margarine

Heat mushroom soup, chicken broth and cheese until melted. Mix with chicken, macaroni and potatoes. Pour in greased pan. Brown bread crumbs with margarine and sprinkle on top of mixture. Bake at 325° for 30 minutes.

Underground Chicken Breast Casserole

Steve & Lorene Helmuth

5 lb. chicken breasts
Runion
¼ c. butter, browned
4 Tbsp. flour, heaping
1 qt. water

½ tsp. seasoning salt
2 tsp. salt
½ pkg. brown gravy mix
Velveeta cheese to taste
6 qt. mashed potatoes

Brown chicken breasts in Runion. Make a gravy with butter, flour, water, seasoned salt and salt. Mix brown gravy mix according to package directions, add to rest of gravy. Add cheese. Add chicken to gravy and pour this mixture into bottom of roaster. Top with prepared mashed potatoes. Drizzle with brown butter. Bake at 325° until heated through.

Bacon Cheeseburger Casserole

Orvan & Marilyn Miller

1 lb. hamburger
¼ c. chopped onions
salt and pepper to taste
½ tsp. garlic (optional)
1 tsp. Worcestershire sauce

1 can cream of celery soup
1 lb. bacon
cooked and shredded potatoes
Velveeta cheese

Brown hamburger and onions together. Add seasonings, Worcestershire sauce and celery soup. Fry bacon. Put a layer of shredded potatoes in a casserole. Top with ½ of meat, then cheese slices, then bacon. Repeat layers. Bake at 400° for 45 minutes. (If making ahead of time do not cover before baking.)

Baked Garlic Red Potatoes

Alvin & Charlene Kanagy

1 c. butter, melted
3 tsp. salt
1 tsp. Lawry's salt
1 tsp. garlic salt

2 Tbsp. parsley
½ tsp. pepper
½ tsp. paprika
4 qt. diced potatoes

Mix seasonings with melted butter; then pour over potatoes. Stir a little until potatoes are well covered, must cover tightly with tin foil. Bake 1½ hours at 350° if you have a large amount. For small amount will be soft in an hour.

Baked Potato Wedges

LaWayne Helmuth

6 lg. potatoes, raw
¼ c. flour
¼ c. grated Parmesan cheese
parsley flakes (optional)

¾ tsp. salt
⅛ tsp. pepper
⅓ c. butter

Pare and slice potatoes. Combine flour, cheese, salt and pepper in a bag. Moisten potatoes with water and shake potatoes in the bag, coating them well. Melt butter in a 9"x13" baking pan. Place potatoes in pan and sprinkle with parsley flakes. Bake at 375° for 1 hour turning once during baking, until golden brown.

Easy Cheesy Potato Casserole

Renita Faye Helmuth

3 qt. cooked and diced potatoes
1½ qt. green beans, cooked and
  drained
3 c. milk
1 tsp. salt

1½ lb. hot dogs, cut up
1 lb. Velveeta cheese
¼ c. flour
1 c. bread crumbs
2 Tbsp. butter

Heat milk, flour and salt until thickened. Stir in cheese to melt. In casserole, mix potatoes, green beans and hot dogs together; pour sauce over everything and top with bread crumbs. Melt butter and drizzle over top. Bake at 375° for approx. 45 minutes.

Note: Toasted bread cubes are good too, on top, instead of bread crumbs.

Easy Cheese Potatoes

Melvin & Beth Ann Beachy

32 oz. frozen hash brown
   potatoes
½ c. butter, melted
1 can cream of mushroom soup

16 oz. sour cream, softened
2 c. shredded cheddar cheese
½ soup can milk

Put the hash browns in a 9"x13" greased baking dish. Pour the melted butter over them. In a bowl mix soup, sour cream, cheese and milk. Pour cheese mixture evenly over the potatoes. Bake at 350° for 1¼ hour, covered.

Potato Haystack Casserole

Willard & Carol Ann Helmuth
Wilmer & Sarah Beachy

8 lb. potatoes, cooked and
   shredded
2 pkg. Hidden Valley Ranch
   dressing mix
2 c. sour cream

2 c. milk
4 lb. hamburger fried with onions
1 or 2 pkg. taco seasoning
salt and pepper to taste
Doritos, crushed

Cheese Sauce:
½ c. butter
¼ c. flour

4 c. milk
1 lb. Velveeta

Mix Ranch dressing mix with sour cream and milk. Add to potatoes. Brown hamburger and onions; add taco seasoning. Put potatoes in bottom of large stainless steel roaster. Put hamburger on top of potatoes. Make cheese sauce and put on top of potatoes. Bake at 350° for 1–1½ hours. Just before serving put crushed Doritos on top. Yield: Serves 40.

Party Mashed Potatoes

Mary Lorene Beachy

10 lb. potatoes
2 tsp. salt
1 tsp. Greek seasoning
8 oz. cream cheese

1 c. sour cream
4 Tbsp. butter
milk as needed

Cook potatoes until tender and mash. Add the rest of the ingredients. Refrigerate. When ready to serve, bake until heated through at 325°. Serves 30.

Potluck Potatoes

Melvin & Beth Ann Beachy

12 lb. potatoes, cooked
   and shredded
½ c. butter
½ c. flour
6 c. milk
3 cans cream of chicken soup

2 c. sour cream
2 tsp. pepper
3 tsp. salt
1¼ lb. Velveeta cheese
6 c. crushed cornflakes mixed
   with ¾ c. melted butter

Put potatoes in a large roaster. (This recipe fills a lifetime roaster.) Melt butter; add flour and blend until smooth. Add milk and blend until boiling. Then over medium heat add chicken soup, sour cream, pepper and salt, stirring occasionally; add Velveeta cheese and stir until cheese melts. Pour over potatoes and cover top with crushed cornflakes mixed with melted butter. Bake for 1½ hours at 350°. May also add ham if you wish. If this is cold, bake for 2 hours. Serves 30.

Potluck Potato Casserole

Orvan & Marilyn Miller

2 lb. boiled potatoes, peeled
   and chopped or shredded
4 Tbsp. butter, melted
1 tsp. salt
¼ tsp. pepper
1 can cream of chicken soup

2 c. sour cream
2 c. grated cheese
½ c. chopped onions
2 c. crushed cornflakes mixed
   with ¼ c. melted butter

Combine potatoes and butter in large mixing bowl. Add salt, pepper, onions, soup, sour cream and cheese. Blend thoroughly. Pour in casserole dish. Cover with crushed cornflakes mixed with melted butter. Bake at 350° for 45 minutes. Crushed white crackers may be used instead of cornflakes.

Potato Ranch Casserole

Wilmer & Sarah Beachy

2–3 lb. hamburger
1 med. onion, chopped
2 cans cream of
   mushroom soup
2 c. sour cream
2 c. Ranch dressing

4 qt. potatoes, cooked and
   shredded
16 oz. mozzarella or
   marble cheese
1 lb. bacon, fried and crumbled

Brown hamburger and onions; add a dash of salt and pepper. Drain. Mix soup and hamburger and place in large roaster. Mix sour cream and dressing, then mix in potatoes. Spread potatoes on top of hamburger. Bake at 325° for 45 minutes or until heated through. Sprinkle cheese and bacon on top and bake until cheese melts. Pepperoni may be used instead of bacon.

Penny Supper

Levi & Katie Beachy

6 hot dogs, sliced
6 med. potatoes, cooked and
    diced
2 Tbsp. onions, cut fine
¼ c. butter

1 pt. peas
1 pt. corn
1 can cream of mushroom soup
salt and pepper to taste

Bake at 350° for 30 minutes.

Shredded Potato Bake

Wilmer & Sarah Beachy

10 med. potatoes, cooked
    and shredded
2 c. peas
1 onion, finely chopped
½ c. margarine

flour
4–6 c. milk
salt to taste
1 c. Velveeta cheese
2 c. sour cream

Melt margarine; add enough flour to make a paste; add enough milk to make a white sauce. Cook until thickened. Add salt and cheese, when melted, remove from heat. Add rest of ingredients. Mix with potatoes, onions and peas. Put in baking dish. Bake at 325°–350° for 1–1½ hours.

Optional: Add cubed ham for extra flavor.

Sausage Potato Casserole

Steve & Lorene Helmuth

1 lb. ground sausage	½ tsp. salt
1 can cream of mushroom soup	¼ tsp. pepper
¾ c. milk	3 c. thinly sliced potatoes
¼ c. chopped onions	4 oz. shredded cheese

Fry sausage; drain. In a bowl combine soup, milk, onions, salt and pepper. In an ungreased 11"x17" baking dish, layer half the potatoes, soup mixture and sausage; repeat layers. Cover and bake at 350° for 1½ hours or until done. Sprinkle with cheese and return to oven until melted.

Sausage Sauerkraut Casserole

Wilmer & Sarah Beachy

1½ lb. sausage, browned and drained	6 med. potatoes
	1 c. sour cream
2 c. sauerkraut	2 c. American cheese slices

Fix potatoes as mashed potatoes. Put sausage in bottom of 3 quart casserole, top with sauerkraut. Spread potatoes over sauerkraut, then next the sour cream. If all ingredients are warm when you layer them, you need to bake only 30 minutes, otherwise it will take longer. Add cheese 5 minutes before it is finished.

Tater Tot Casserole

Orvan & Marilyn Miller

2 lb. hamburger   cheese
2 cans cream of mushroom soup   tater tots
1 can of milk

Brown hamburger; add mushroom soup and milk. Put in casserole, top with cheese and tater tots. Bake at 350° until heated through. About 45–60 minutes.

Note: I add very little salt and pepper. Then I add hickory smoke salt.

Underground Ham Casserole

Levi & Katie Beachy

5 c. cubed ham, cooked   1 c. milk
4 Tbsp. butter   2 c. Velveeta cheese
½ c. diced onions   4 qt. mashed potatoes
1 Tbsp. Worcestershire sauce   2 c. sour cream
2 cans cream of mushroom soup   1 lb. bacon, fried and crumbled

Combine butter, ham, onions and Worcestershire sauce, cook until onions are tender. Put in bottom of roaster. Heat milk, soup, and cheese until cheese melts. Place on top of first layer. Mash potatoes, using no milk only sour cream. Spread on ham. Put crumbled bacon on top of all. Bake at 350° for 20 minutes or until heated through. Serves 25 people.

Beachy Family Favorites

Sweet Potato Casserole

Wilmer & Sarah Beachy

3 c. sweet potatoes, cooked and mashed
½ c. margarine

1 c. sugar
2 eggs
1 tsp. vanilla

Topping:
1 c. brown sugar
½ c. flour

⅓ c. margarine, softened
1 c. chopped nuts

Mix sweet potatoes, sugar, margarine, eggs and vanilla. Put in buttered baking dish. Pour topping over potatoes and sprinkle 1 cup nuts on top. Bake covered at 350° for 25 minutes.

Garden Skillet

Raymond & Martha Beachy

1 sm. head cauliflower, separated into florets
2 med. zucchini, sliced
1 med. green bell pepper, cut into strips
1 sm. onion, sliced
3 Tbsp. butter, melted
2 tomatoes, cut into wedges

1 tsp. dried basil
1 tsp. dried oregano
¾ tsp. salt
1 lg. clove garlic, peeled and crushed
¼ tsp. pepper
3 Tbsp. Parmesan cheese, divided

Cook first 4 ingredients in butter in a large skillet, stirring constantly, 4–5 minutes or until crisp-tender. Add tomatoes, seasonings and 2 tablespoons Parmesan cheese; cook over medium heat 1 minute tossing gently. Transfer to serving dish; sprinkle with remaining Parmesan cheese. May use other variety of veggies.

Onion Patties

Orvan & Marilyn Miller

¾ c. flour

1 Tbsp. sugar

1 Tbsp. cornmeal

2½ c. finely chopped onions

2 tsp. baking powder

1 tsp. salt

¾ c. milk

Mix well and fry in vegetable oil.

Quick Green Beans

Abner & Sovilla Mae Zook

1 qt. canned green beans

2 Tbsp. butter

2 Tbsp. sour cream and onion
   powder

In saucepan, melt butter. Add green beans and simmer 10 minutes. Add seasoning and stir well.

Scalloped Squash

Wilmer & Sarah Beachy

3 pt. raw squash, sliced

1 onion, diced

1 c. cream

2 tsp. salt

1 qt. bread crumbs, toasted
   with butter

Put half of squash in baking dish, then half of onions, salt and crumbs. Add remaining squash, onions and salt. Pour cream over all and add remaining crumbs. Bake at 350° for 45 minutes or more, until done.

Note: We omit the bread crumbs and use sliced American cheese.

Huntington Chicken

Steve & Lorene Helmuth

4 lb. chicken	½ c. cheese
2 c. shell macaroni	4 c. buttered bread crumbs
4 c. chicken broth	½ c. cream (optional)
½ c. flour	

Stew chicken, then cut in cubes. Cook macaroni in salt water. Drain and cool in cold water and drain again. Thicken broth and mix. Add cut-up cheese. Spread in greased pans. Sprinkle with buttered crumbs. Brown in oven at 350° for 30–60 minutes.

Hearty Hamburger Casserole

Treva Kay Beachy

3 lb. hamburger	2 cans cream of mushroom soup
3 onions, sliced	9 slices bacon
3 c. sliced potatoes	1 qt. tomato juice
3 c. diced celery	1 lb. cheddar cheese
3 c. cooked spaghetti	

Brown hamburger and onions. Drain and pour into a casserole dish. Layer the potatoes, celery and spaghetti. Pour the mushroom soup over the mixture. Fry the bacon and cut into small pieces and put on top. Pour tomato juice over the bacon and then sprinkle the cheese over the top. Cover and bake at 350° for 1½ hours.

Hamburger Helper

Orvan & Marilyn Miller

1 lb. ground beef
chopped onions
2 c. hot water
1½ c. macaroni
1 tsp. salt

pepper to taste
1½ tsp. chili powder
1¼ tsp. celery seed (optional)
Velveeta cheese
1 can cream of mushroom soup

Brown ground beef and onions in pan. Add hot water and seasonings. When water boils, stir in macaroni. Simmer until macaroni is soft. Stir occasionally. Add about ½ lb. cheese and mushroom soup. Serve when cheese is melted.

Noodle Casserole

Levi & Katie Beachy

1 lb. noodles, cooked
1 lb. browned hamburger,
  seasoned with salt and pepper

1 qt. corn, cooked
2 cans cream of mushroom soup
cheese

Mix all ingredients together, put into casserole and heat until bubbly.

Sausage Supreme

Orvan & Marilyn Miller

1 lb. pork sausage
1 onion, chopped or
   1 tsp. minced onions
1 can cream of mushroom soup

½ c. milk
1 c. diced cheese
8–12 oz. fine noodles

Fry sausage long enough to fry out fat, but not until crisp. Drain well. Fry onions. Cook noodles and drain. Mix all ingredients together in casserole dish and bake at 325° for 25–35 minutes.

Yumesetti Casserole

Omer & Dorothy Beachy

1 lb. noodles
3 lb. hamburger
1 onion or 2 Tbsp. onion flakes
½ loaf of bread
4–6 Tbsp. margarine

2 cans cream of mushroom soup
2 cans cream of celery soup
2 c. sour cream
1 pt. peas or corn

Cook noodles in salt water until done. Fry hamburger and onions. Break or cut bread to small cubes and brown in skillet with margarine. Mix all soups, sour cream and vegetables. Then mix it with noodles, hamburger and ½ of bread cubes. Put in casserole and put remaining cubes on top. Bake at 350° for 1 hour.

Note: I do not put any bread cubes in my casserole, just on top. They get too soggy.

Cheesy Baked Beans

Alvin & Charlene Kanagy

2 (16 oz.) cans pork and beans   1 Tbsp. mustard
½ tsp. chili powder   1 c. shredded Colby cheese
2 Tbsp. brown sugar

   Preheat oven to 350°. Combine all ingredients except cheese. Pour into a 1½ quart casserole and bake until hot and bubbly. Sprinkle cheese on top and bake until melted.

Sauce for Baked Beans

Abner & Sovilla Mae Zook

9 c. brown sugar   2¼ c. mustard
9 c. ketchup   ½ c. chili powder
2¼ c. dried onions   1 c. Worcestershire sauce

   Mix all ingredients together. Mix 2 cups sauce to 1 gallon Bush Baked Beans. To Can: Cold Pack 30 minutes.
   Note: (Optional) Add 2 cups hot dogs to every gallon of beans.

> *To clean and soften hands after gardening or field work, wash them with pure apple cider vinegar.*

Beachy Family Favorites

Lasagna
Orvan & Marilyn Miller

3½–4 lb. hamburger
1–2 onions
1 qt. pizza sauce
10 lasagna noodles, cooked 10 min.

2 eggs, beat and put in cottage cheese
2 (24 oz.) cottage cheese
2 pkg. shredded cheese

Fry hamburger and onions, drain off fat. Put in pizza sauce. Sprinkle a little hamburger on bottom of casserole. Then put in a layer of noodles, then a layer of meat, a layer of cottage cheese, then shredded cheese. Start with noodles again and so on until all is gone. End with shredded cheese on top. Makes a large casserole. (Sometimes I have too many noodles.) Bake at 350° until done, about 45 minutes.

Creamy Beef Lasagna
Marnita Beachy

1½ lb. ground beef
1 qt. pizza sauce
¼ c. chopped onions
2 tsp. sugar
2 tsp. salt
2 tsp. Worcestershire sauce
½ tsp. garlic salt

16 oz. cream cheese, softened
1 c. sour cream
¼ c. milk
18 lasagna noodles, cooked and drained
1 c. shredded cheese

Cook beef until no longer pink. Drain. Stir in pizza sauce, onions, sugar, salt, Worcestershire sauce and garlic salt. In a mixing bowl, beat cream cheese, sour cream and milk until smooth. In a greased 9"x13" pan, layer a fourth of the meat sauce, six noodles and ⅓ of cheese mixture. Repeat layers twice. Top with remaining meat sauce. Cover and bake at 350° for 40 minutes. Uncover; sprinkle with cheddar cheese. Bake 5 minutes longer or until cheese is melted. Let set 15 minutes before cutting. Yield: 12 servings.

Mexican Lasagna

Raymond & Martha Beachy

1 lb. hamburger
16 oz. can refried beans
2 tsp. oregano
1 tsp. ground cumin
¾ tsp. garlic powder
12 uncooked lasagna noodles
2½ c. water

2½ c. salsa
2 c. sour cream
¾ c. chopped onions
2 oz. sliced black olives
1 c. shredded Monterey
   Jack cheese

Combine fried hamburger, beans and spices. Place 4 of the uncooked noodles in the bottom of a 9"x13" pan. Spread half the meat mixture over noodles. Top with 4 more noodles and remaining meat mixture. Cover with remaining noodles. Combine water with salsa. Pour over all; cover tightly with foil; bake at 350° for 1½ hour or until noodles are tender. Combine sour cream, onions and olives. Spoon over casserole; top with cheese. Bake uncovered until cheese melts, about 5–10 minutes.

To clean stainless steel cookware that has been stained from cooking vegetables, add a little lemon juice. They will be sparkling clean with no scrubbing.

Delicious Pizza Casserole

Willard & Carol Ann Helmuth
Steven & Lorene Helmuth

Crust:

1⅓ c. flour

⅔ tsp. salt

¼ c. vegetable oil

2 tsp. baking powder

½ c. milk

Topping:

2 lb. sausage or hamburger, fried

1 c. spaghetti, cooked and
   drained

1 pt. pizza sauce

1 c. sour cream

3 Tbsp. salad dressing

3 c. shredded cheese

Mix crust ingredients and pat in bottom of a 9"x13" pan. Put meat on top of dough, and spaghetti on top of meat. Spread pizza sauce over spaghetti. Mix sour cream and salad dressing and put on top of pizza sauce; cover with grated cheese and (pepperoni, optional). Bake at 350° until crust is brown.

Pizza

Orvan & Marilyn Miller

Crust:

1 c. flour	1 Tbsp. sugar
1 tsp. baking powder	¼ c. shortening or margarine
¼ tsp. cream of tartar	1 egg
¼ tsp. salt	⅓ c. milk

Topping:

2 lb. hamburger or	mushrooms
1 lb. hamburger and	1 can cream of mushroom soup
1 lb. sausage, fried	12–16 oz. pizza sauce
salt and pepper	cheese
onions	pepperoni
peppers	

Mix dry ingredients and cut in shortening or margarine, until mixture resembles coarse crumbs. Pour milk in slowly. Add egg and stir well. May need to add a little more flour. Divide evenly onto 2 pizza pans. Top with fried hamburger. Add salt and pepper, onions, peppers, mushrooms and whatever else you wish. Add cream of mushroom soup and pizza sauce. Mix well. Divide evenly on 2 pizza pans. Bake at 350° for 30 minutes or until almost done. Then top with cheese and pepperoni.

Pizza Supreme

Alvin & Charlene Kanagy

Crust:

1 pkg. dry yeast
1 c. warm water
1 tsp. sugar

1 tsp. salt
2 Tbsp. vegetable oil
2½ c. bread flour

Toppings:

sausage
ham
pepperoni
mushrooms
hamburger

bacon
peppers
1 lb. shredded cheese
1 pt. pizza sauce

Dissolve yeast in water and sugar. Add rest of dough ingredients and knead until smooth, let set 5 minutes. Press on greased cookie sheet, sprinkled with yellow cornmeal. Bake crust lightly 8–10 minutes. Remove from oven, spread with pizza sauce, put on toppings. Return to 375° and finish baking for 15–20 minutes or until thoroughly hot and cheese is melted.

Grilled Chicken Club Pizza

Alvin & Charlene Kanagy

11"x17" pizza crust
3 boneless, skinless
   chicken breasts
⅓ c. Italian dressing
⅔ c. sour cream

¾ c. Ranch dressing
½ lb. fried bacon
¼ c. Parmesan cheese
mozzarella cheese

Cut chicken breasts into cubes and cook in Italian dressing until browned. Mix sour cream and Ranch dressing; spread on slightly pre-baked crust, cover with Parmesan cheese, chicken and bacon. Bake at 400° until done and top with mozzarella cheese.

Pizza Pie Dough

Melvin & Beth Ann Beachy

1 Tbsp. yeast	1 Tbsp. vegetable oil
1 c. warm water	1 tsp. salt
1 Tbsp. sugar	2¼ c. flour

Mix together yeast, sugar and warm water. Then add rest of ingredients. Work out into pan with oiled hands.

Burritos

Willard & Carol Ann Helmuth

2 lb. hamburger	lettuce
salt and pepper	tomatoes
1 pkg. taco seasoning	cheddar cheese
1 c. water	sour cream
16 oz. taco sauce	Super Salad Dressing
16 flour tortillas	

Fry hamburger; add salt, pepper, water, taco seasoning and taco sauce. Simmer 15 minutes. Heat tortillas; put lettuce, hamburger, tomatoes, cheese, sour cream and dressing on tortillas. Roll up and enjoy. Serves 16.

Burrito Casserole

Wesley & Martha Beachy

1½–2 lb. hamburger
1 lg. can refried beans
¼ c. water
1 pkg. taco seasoning

2 cans cream of mushroom soup
½ c. sour cream
7–8 flour tortillas
shredded cheese

Brown hamburger; drain. Add beans, water and taco seasoning. Mix soup and sour cream. Put half of soup mixture into 9"x13" pan. Fill tortillas with meat and bean mixture, roll shut and place on top of soup. Pour rest of soup mixture over burritos. Cover and bake at 350° for 1 hour. Top with shredded cheese. Serve with chopped lettuce and tomatoes, salsa and sour cream.

Wet Burrito Casserole

Christopher & Theresa Gingerich

1½ c. sour cream
1 can cream of mushroom soup
2 lb. hamburger
1 med. green pepper, diced
1 med. onion, chopped

1 pkg. taco seasoning mix
1 sm. can mushrooms, diced
16 oz. refried beans
4 c. shredded cheese
1 pkg. soft tortilla shells

Mix sour cream and mushroom soup. Put half of mixture in bottom of 9"x13" pan. Fry hamburger, onion and green pepper. Add mushrooms, taco seasoning and beans to hamburger and heat. Divide mixture onto tortilla shells (approx. 10). Roll up shells and place on top of sour cream mixture in pan. Top with remaining sour cream and soup mixture. Sprinkle with cheese. Bake at 350° for 30 minutes.

Wet Burrito Casserole

Willard & Carol Ann Helmuth

1 can cream of mushroom soup
2 c. sour cream
1 lg. can refried beans
1 lb. hamburger, browned

1 pkg. taco seasoning
6-8" flour tortillas
½ c. shredded cheddar cheese

Combine mushroom soup and sour cream. Combine browned hamburger with taco seasoning and refried beans in another bowl. Spread meat mixture on tortillas. Roll up and put in a 9"x13" pan. Pour soup mixture on top and sprinkle with cheese. Bake at 350° for 30 minutes. Serves 6 to 8 people.

Cheesy Enchiladas

Melvin & Beth Ann Beachy

Cheese Sauce:
¼ c. flour
3 c. milk
½ c. margarine

8 oz. Velveeta cheese
1 c. sour cream
salt to taste

Meat Mixture:
2 lb. hamburger, browned
1 med. onion, minced
1 can kidney beans

1 pkg. taco seasoning
12 flour tortillas

Cheese Sauce: Bring flour and milk to boiling point then turn off heat and add rest of ingredients. Place meat mixture in tortilla. Roll up and place in buttered baking dish. Pour cheese sauce over top. Bake at 350° until cheese starts to bubble and turn brown. Serve plain or with shredded lettuce, chopped tomatoes and salsa.

Beachy Family Favorites

Stromboli

Wilmer & Sarah Beachy

Dough:

1⅓ c. warm water
1 Tbsp. yeast
2 Tbsp. vegetable oil

½ tsp. salt
4–5 c. flour

Filling:

pizza sauce
hamburger or sausage, browned
peppers
onions

mushrooms
pepperoni
mozzarella cheese

Dissolve yeast in water, then mix with rest of ingredients same as bread dough. Let rise. Divide dough into 3 parts and roll ¼" thick. Spread pizza sauce over dough. Layer the meat, vegetables and cheese on one half of each piece of dough. Fold over edges and press together. Brush butter on top and sprinkle with seasoned salt. Bake at 350° for 25 minutes. Let set for 10–15 minutes before serving. Cut and serve. Any kind of meat may be used.

Taco Bake

Marnita Beachy

2 c. Bisquick
⅔ c. milk
2 lb. hamburger
2 pkg. taco seasoning mix
1 c. sour cream

1 c. mayonnaise
2 c. shredded cheese
lettuce
tomatoes
salsa

Mix Bisquick and milk, put in 9"x13" pan. Mix hamburger and taco seasoning. Put on top of dough. Combine sour cream and mayonnaise, put on top of meat. Bake at 350° approx. 20 minutes (or until crust is finished). Top with shredded cheese, bake until cheese is melted. Serve with lettuce, tomatoes and salsa.

Taco Casserole

Melvin & Beth Ann Beachy

2 lb. hamburger, fried
2 Tbsp. minced onions
2 pkg. taco seasoning
2 cans cream of mushroom soup

1 can cream of chicken soup
1 pkg. nacho chips, crushed
1 pkg. cheddar cheese

Mix together hamburger, onions, seasoning and soups. Pour into casserole dishes. Put nacho chips in bottom of pan. Top with cheese when almost done baking. Bake at 300° for 30–35 minutes.

Chicken Dressing

Melvin & Beth Ann Beachy

2 qt. chicken broth with
    chicken pieces
2 qt. boiling water
3 loaves bread, cubed
10 eggs, beaten
1½ c. milk

1 c. finely chopped celery
3 tsp. salt
3 Tbsp. chicken seasoning
2 Tbsp. parsley flakes
2 tsp. pepper
1 c. butter, browned

Heat chicken broth and water and pour over bread and stir well; add eggs and milk and rest of ingredients and mix well again. Spray pans with cooking spray before filling. I like to use glass pans. Fills 3 regular size glass pans or a little over 2 large size pans. Bake at 350° for 1 hour. Serves 70.

Chicken Dressing

Nelson Zook

12 c. bread	⅛ tsp. pepper
½ c. butter	1 tsp. salt
2 eggs, beaten	1 tsp. chicken seasoning
1 c. celery	1 Tbsp. parsley flakes
1 sm. onion	1 qt. chicken pieces

Brown bread in melted butter. Mix all together, may need to add some broth if too dry. Bake at 350° for 1 hour.

Ranch Chicken Bake

Alvin & Charlene Kanagy

¾ c. Ranch dressing	4 chicken breasts
2 Tbsp. flour	cheddar cheese

Mix Ranch dressing and flour together; dip chicken breasts in Ranch mixture and put in casserole dish. Sprinkle cheddar cheese over it. Bake at 350° for 20–25 minutes.

> To strain cooking oil after deep-fat frying, place a paper coffee filter in the funnel used to pour the oil back into the jar. Then just throw the filter away.

Chicken Gumbo

Melvin & Beth Ann Beachy

9 slices bread
4 c. cooked chicken
4 eggs, beaten
1 c. chicken broth
1 c. milk

1 tsp. salt
9 slices Velveeta cheese
2 cans cream of celery or
    cream of mushroom soup

Spray casserole dish with cooking spray. Put bread slices in bottom of casserole dish. Put chicken on top of bread. Mix eggs, broth, milk and salt. Pour this over bread and chicken. Cover with cheese slices, then soup on top of cheese. Brown bread crumbs in ¼ cup butter. Spread crumbs on top of casserole. Bake uncovered at 350° for 1¼ hours.

Mock Turkey

Levi & Katie Beachy

2 lb. ground beef, fried
2 cans cream of chicken soup
1 can cream of celery soup

4 c. milk
20 oz. loaf bread, cubed
salt and pepper to taste

Mix all together and place in pan. Bake at 350° for 1 hour.

Haystacks

Levi Beachy Family

1 lb. Ritz crackers, crushed
4 c. prepared rice,
   cooked in salt water
2 heads lettuce, cut up
12 med. tomatoes
hamburger stew

2½ c. diced celery
2½ c. shredded carrots
2½ c. sunflower seeds
1 bag corn chips, crushed
cheese sauce

Stew:
4 lb. ground beef
4 cans tomatoes
4 cans kidney beans
¾ c. chili powder

8 bay leaves
1 c. minced onions
8 c. water
salt

Cheese Sauce 1:
2 cans cheddar cheese soup

1 can milk

Or Cheese Sauce 2:
3 qt. milk
1 Tbsp. salt

1½–2 lb. Velveeta cheese
1½ c. flour

Stew: Combine all ingredients. Simmer 1½ hours or until thick. We usually use our own tomato juice or V-8 juice. To serve, stack on plate in order of – crackers, rice, lettuce, chopped tomatoes, stew, celery, carrots, sunflower seeds, corn chips and cheese sauce.
Cheese Sauce 1: Use 2 cans cheddar cheese soup to 1 can of milk. Heat.
Cheese Sauce 2: Or use milk, salt, Velveeta cheese and flour. Heat until thickened. Be careful, it scorches easily. Serves 14.

Cakes & Frostings

A Love Cake for Mother

1 can of obedience
several lbs. of affection
1 pt. of neatness
some holiday, birthday and everyday surprises
1 can of 'running errands' (willing brand)
1 box powdered 'get up when I should'
1 bottle of 'keep sunny all day long'
1 can of 'pure thoughtfulness'

Mix well, bake in a hearty warm oven and serve to Mother every day. She ought to have it in big slices.

Yellow Chiffon Cake

Levi & Katie Beachy

2¼ c. sifted flour	½ c. milk
1 c. sugar	1½ tsp. vanilla
1 Tbsp. baking powder	½ c. milk
1 tsp. salt	2 egg yolks
⅓ c. vegetable oil or	2 egg whites
softened butter	½ c. sugar

Sift together flour, sugar, baking powder and salt. Add vegetable oil, ½ c. milk and vanilla. Beat 1 minute, then add another ½ cup milk and egg yolks. Beat 1 minute more then fold in a very stiff meringue of: 2 egg whites and ½ cup sugar. Bake at 350° for 40–50 minutes in a 9"x13" pan.

Chocolate Chip Chiffon Cake
Levi & Katie Beachy

Follow recipe for Yellow Chiffon; after adding mcringue, add 2 oz. (¼ cup) grated chocolate.

Angel Food Cake
Raymond & Martha Beachy

1¾ c. egg whites
1½ tsp. cream of tartar
¼ tsp. salt

1¼ c. cake flour
2 c. sugar

For flavored cakes, add 2 rounded tablespoons Jell-O: for chocolate reduce flour to 1 cup and add ¼ cup cocoa. Sift flour and sugar (also Jell-O or cocoa if desired) and set aside. Beat egg whites, cream of tartar and salt until stiff peaks form; fold in sifted ingredients and bake at 375° for 45 minutes.

Angel Food Cake*
Beachy's Bulk Foods

¾ c. sugar
1½ c. cake flour
2 c. egg whites

1 Tbsp. cream of tartar
¼ tsp. salt
1 tsp. vanilla

Measure and sift together sugar and cake flour. Put egg whites, cream of tartar, salt and vanilla into a large bowl; beat until foamy. Add gradually (2 Tbsp. at a time) ¾ cup additional sugar. Beat after each addition until firm and holds stiff peaks. Fold in flour mixture. (Using a plastic spatula works best.) Bake at 350° for about 35 minutes or until it is browned nicely and springs back when touched lightly.

Flavored Angel Food Cake*

Beachy's Bulk Foods

For strawberry, blackberry, apricot, etc.: Use that flavor Jell-O and add 3 tablespoons Jell-O to your flour and sugar mixture.

Lemon: Add 1 teaspoon lemon flavoring and yellow food coloring, until the desired color is reached.

Chocolate: Add 3 tablespoons sifted cocoa.

Butter Pecan: Add 1 teaspoon butter pecan flavoring and ½ cup pecans.

Black Walnut: Add 2 teaspoons black walnut flavoring and ½ cup black walnuts.

Chocolate and Cherry Chip: Add ½ cup chips. Any flavor chips may be used, also.

Coconut: Add 1 teaspoon coconut flavoring and ½ cup coconut.

Note: In any flavor you choose always add flavorings, chips, etc. into the batter along with flour and sugar mixture.

Chocolate Angel Food Cake

Wilmer & Sarah Beachy

2 c. + 2 Tbsp. egg whites	1 c. white sugar
1½ tsp. cream of tartar	1 c. cocoa
1 tsp. salt	½ c. Softasilk cake flour

Sift together white sugar, cocoa and cake flour. Beat egg whites, cream of tartar and salt until frothy; add 1 additional cup white sugar. Beat until stiff peaks start to form. Do not beat too stiff. Fold sifted flour/cocoa mixture in egg whites, gently and slowly in three parts, 20–25 whips for each addition. Bake at 350° for 45–50 minutes.

Note: Have all ingredients at room temperature.

Amish Cake

Jeremy Helmuth

½ c. butter
2 c. brown sugar
3 c. flour

2 c. buttermilk
2 tsp. soda
2 tsp. vanilla

Topping:
6 Tbsp. butter, melted
1 c. brown sugar
¼ c. milk

½ c. coconut
½ c. nuts

Mix butter and sugar together. Add rest of ingredients and flour alternately. Bake at 375° in a 9"x13" pan. Mix together topping ingredients and spread on top of hot cake. Put back in oven until light brown.

Apple Dapple Cake

Levi & Katie Beachy

2 eggs
2 c. white sugar
1 c. Wesson oil
3 c. flour, scant
½ tsp. salt

1 tsp. soda
3 c. chopped apples
2 tsp. vanilla
nuts

Icing:
1 c. brown sugar
¼ c. milk

¼ c. margarine

Mix eggs, sugar and Wesson oil. Add sifted dry ingredients; then add apples, vanilla and nuts. Bake at 350° for 45 minutes or until done. *Icing:* Cook 2½ minutes. Stir a little after removing from stove, then pour over cake while still hot.

Superior Apple Cake

Wilmer & Sarah Beachy

1 c. shortening
2 c. sugar
2 eggs
3 c. flour
2 tsp. soda
¾ tsp. salt

2 tsp. cinnamon
2 tsp. vanilla
1 tsp. black walnut flavor
1 c. prepared coffee
4 c. peeled and diced apples

Topping:
⅔ c. brown sugar

½ c. black walnuts or pecans

Cream shortening, sugar and eggs. Add dry ingredients alternately with coffee. Add apples. *Topping:* Mix together and put on top of cake before baking. Bake in a 9"x13" pan until done.

Roman Apple Cake

Steven & Lorene Helmuth

1 c. white sugar
½ c. brown sugar
1 c. vegetable oil
2 eggs
1 c. sour milk
2½ c. flour

1 tsp. baking powder
1 tsp. soda
2 tsp. cinnamon
½ tsp. salt
2 c. raw, shredded apples

Topping:
½ c. white sugar
1 tsp. cinnamon

½ c. nuts

Cream together the sugars and vegetable oil; add eggs and beat. Mix together flour, baking powder, soda, cinnamon and salt and add alternately with the milk. Pour into a 9"x13" cake pan. *Topping:* Mix white sugar, cinnamon and nuts together. Sprinkle on top of cake before baking. Bake at 350° for 30–40 minutes.

Beachy Family Favorites

Caramel Apple Cake

Raymond & Martha Beachy

3 eggs
2 c. sugar
1½ c. vegetable oil
2 tsp. vanilla
3 c. flour

1 tsp. salt
1 tsp. soda
3 c. chopped apples
1 c. chopped pecans

Topping:
½ c. butter
¼ c. milk

1 c. brown sugar
pinch of salt

Beat eggs until foamy. Gradually add sugar; then blend in vegetable oil and vanilla. Combine flour, salt and soda. Add to egg mixture. Stir in pecans and apples. Pour into a greased 10" tube pan. Bake at 350° for 1¼ hour or until done. Cool 10 minutes on wire rack, then remove to a serving platter. Pour topping slowly over warm cake. *Topping:* Combine all ingredients in saucepan and boil for 3 minutes.

> *For easy cake removal: Rinse a towel with cold water. Remove cake from oven and place on towel for a few minutes. Remove cake from pan.*

Banana Chiffon Cake

Levi & Katie Beachy

2 c. sifted flour
1 c. sugar
1 tsp. baking powder
1 tsp. soda
1 tsp. salt
⅓ c. vegetable oil

1 c. mashed bananas, very ripe
⅔ c. buttermilk or sour
  milk, divided
1 tsp. vanilla
2 egg yolks

Meringue:
2 egg whites   ⅓ c. sugar

Sift together flour, sugar, baking powder, soda and salt into a bowl; add vegetable oil, bananas, ⅓ c. buttermilk or sour milk and vanilla. Beat 1 minute; then add another ⅓ cup buttermilk and egg yolks. Beat 1 minute more, then add very stiff beaten meringue. Gently fold in ½ cup chopped nuts, if desired. Pour in a 9"x13" pan. Bake at 350° for 40–45 minutes.

Soft Banana Cake

Melvin & Beth Ann Beachy

1 yellow cake mix
1 c. mashed bananas with
  1 tsp. soda added

1 Tbsp. flour, heaping

Mix cake mix as directed on box; plus add the rest of the ingredients. Beat well. Bake in a 9"x13" pan at 350° until done.

Blackberry Jam Cake

Abner & Sovilla Mae Zook

2 c. sugar
2 c. butter
6 eggs
1 c. pecans
1 c. black walnuts
2 c. blackberry jam

1 c. buttermilk
1 tsp. soda
4 c. flour
2 tsp. cinnamon
1 tsp. allspice
1 tsp. nutmeg

Add soda to buttermilk. Cream sugar and butter; add beaten eggs, jams and nuts. Bake at 275° for 1¾ hour. If using a tube pan, bake at 325°.

Butter Pecan Frosting
(For Butter Pecan Cake)

Raymond & Martha Beachy

3 Tbsp. butter
3 Tbsp. milk
⅓ c. toasted pecans

3 c. powdered sugar
butter pecan flavoring to taste

Cream butter and powdered sugar. Add milk and flavoring. May need to add more milk. Add toasted pecans.

Butter Pecan Cake

Raymond & Martha Beachy

3 Tbsp. butter, melted
1⅓ c. chopped pecans
⅔ c. butter, softened
1⅓ c. sugar
2 eggs
2 c. flour

1½ tsp. baking powder
¼ tsp. salt
⅔ c. milk
1½ tsp. vanilla
1 tsp. butter pecan flavoring

Pour 3 tablespoons melted butter into baking pan. Stir in pecans and toast at 350° for 10 minutes. Set aside to cool. In a bowl cream butter and sugar until light and fluffy. Add eggs one at a time, beating after each addition. Combine flour, baking powder and salt. Add to creamed mixture alternately with milk, beginning and ending with dry ingredients. Stir in flavoring and toasted pecans. Put in 2 rounded greased and floured pans. Bake at 350° for 30–35 minutes.

Butter Sponge Cake

Raymond & Martha Beachy

2 c. sifted cake flour
2 tsp. baking powder
½ c. butter, melted
1 tsp. vanilla

1 c. milk, scalded
12 egg yolks (or 1 c.)
2 c. sugar

Sift together flour and baking powder; add butter and vanilla to scalded milk and keep hot. Beat egg yolks until thick and lemon colored. Gradually beat in sugar; quickly add flour mixture, stir just until mixed. Gently stir in milk mixture. Bake in a greased 9"x13" pan at 350° for 45 minutes or until toothpick inserted comes out clean.

Chocolate Caramel Cake

Alvin & Charlene Kanagy

1 chocolate cake mix
1 can sweetened
  condensed milk

½ can caramel ice cream topping
whipped topping
Butterfinger crumbs

Bake chocolate cake as directed on box. After done take a spoon handle and punch holes in cake. Spread sweetened condensed milk and caramel ice cream topping over top. When cooled, put whipped topping on cake; drizzle with caramel topping and sprinkle with Butterfinger crumbs. Enjoy!

Chips of Chocolate Peanut Butter Cake

Raymond & Martha Beachy

2¼ c. flour
2 c. brown sugar
1 c. peanut butter
½ c. butter, softened
3 eggs

1 c. milk
1 tsp. vanilla
1 tsp. baking powder
½ tsp. soda
1 c. chocolate chips

Mix together flour, brown sugar, peanut butter and butter. Reserve 1 cup. Combine all ingredients and pour batter into a greased 9"x13" pan. Sprinkle reserved crumbs on top and then sprinkle chocolate chips on top of crumbs.

Chocolate Bavarian Torté Cake

Melvin & Beth Ann Beachy

1 chocolate cake mix

Topping:

8 oz. cream cheese

⅔ c. brown sugar

1 tsp. vanilla

⅛ tsp. salt

2 c. whipped topping

2 Tbsp. grated semisweet
    chocolate

Mix cake mix as directed on package and bake in (2) 9" round pans. Cool and split each cake in half. Beat cream cheese, sugar, vanilla and salt. Fold in topping. Spread ¼ in each layer and sprinkle with chocolate. Refrigerate 8 hours or overnight.

Swiss Roll Cake

Treva Kay Beachy

1st Layer:

chocolate cake

2nd Layer:

8 oz. cream cheese, softened

1½ c. powdered sugar

2 Tbsp. pasteurized milk

8 oz. Cool Whip

3rd Layer:

5 Tbsp. butter

1½ c. milk chocolate chips.

1st Layer: Bake a chocolate cake in a sheet pan. *2nd Layer:* Beat cream cheese and powdered sugar; add milk and beat again. Add Cool Whip. Spread on top of cooled cake. Refrigerate 15–20 minutes. *3rd Layer:* Heat butter until melted, but not too hot. Add chocolate chips; stir until melted, then spread evenly over 2nd layer. You will need to work fast and carefully as it will get hard.

Chocolate Fantasy Cake

Marnita Beachy

1 chocolate fudge cake mix	1 Tbsp. prepared coffee
1⅓ c. water	4 eggs
⅓ c. vegetable oil	

Chocolate Mocha Mousse:

¾ c. heavy whipping cream, divided	⅓ c. prepared coffee
	1 c. semisweet chocolate chips
2 Tbsp. sugar	2 tsp. vanilla

Chocolate Whipped Cream Frosting:

1½ c. heavy whipping cream	⅓ c. Dutch process baking cocoa
1¼ c. powdered sugar	½ tsp. vanilla

Beat cake mix, water, vegetable oil, coffee and eggs on low speed 1 minute, scraping bowl constantly. Pour in (3) 8 or 9" pans, 1½ cup in each. Bake about 20 minutes or until done. Cool 10 minutes, then remove from pans and cool completely. *Chocolate Mocha Mousse:* Mix ¼ cup cream, sugar and coffee in 2 quart saucepan. Cook over medium heat, stirring constantly until dissolved and mixture simmers. Stir in chocolate chips with wire whisk until melted. Stir in vanilla. Cool until room temperature. Beat remaining ½ cup cream until soft peaks form. Fold onto chocolate mixture. Cover and refrigerate 30 minutes. Place one cake layer on plate, spread with ½ mousse mixture. Repeat with second layer. Top with remaining layer. *Frosting:* Beat all ingredients in chilled bowl until soft peaks form. Frost side and top of cake with frosting. Cover and refrigerate at least 2 hours before serving. Store covered in refrigerator.

Cream Filled Coffee Cake

Lavon Helmuth

1¼ c. milk
¼ c. butter
⅓ c. sugar
1 Tbsp. salt
1½ Tbsp. yeast

¼ c. lukewarm water
1 tsp. sugar
5½–6 c. flour, divided
3 eggs, well beaten

Streusel Topping:
¼ c. sugar
¼ c. brown sugar
2 Tbsp. flour

2 tsp. cinnamon
¼ c. butter

Cream Filling:
2 egg whites, beaten
2 c. powdered sugar
2 tsp. vanilla

1½ c. Crisco
pecans (optional)

Heat milk, butter, ⅓ c. sugar and salt; stir until sugar dissolves. Set aside. Mix yeast, warm water and 1 teaspoon sugar in a large bowl, let set 10 minutes. Combine 3 cups flour, milk mixture, yeast and eggs, beat until smooth. Add rest of flour to form a soft dough. Cover and let rise 1–1½ hours. *Streusel Topping:* Mix sugars, flour and cinnamon in a bowl. Cut butter into dry ingredients. Set aside. Punch dough down and divide in half. Pat each half into a greased round pan. With a fork pierce entire cake top. Divide topping and sprinkle over each cake. Let rise for about 1 hour. Bake at 350° for 20–25 minutes. Remove from pans and cool. Cut each cake in half and fill with filling. *Filling:* Beat egg whites and stir in powdered sugar and vanilla. Add Crisco. Stir until fluffy. Pecans may be sprinkled on filling before putting the cut off piece on top again.

Yellow Coffee Cake

Darren Zook

1 yellow cake mix
1 Tbsp. flour
1 box instant butterscotch
  pudding
1 tsp. vanilla
4 eggs

½ c. vegetable oil
1 c. water
1 c. chopped nuts
1 c. brown sugar
1 tsp. cinnamon

Mix everything together except nuts, sugar and cinnamon. In separate bowl mix nuts, brown sugar and cinnamon. Sprinkle half of nut mixture in bottom of a 9"x13" cake pan. Pour cake batter over it. Sprinkle remaining crumbs on top. Bake at 375° for 20 minutes, then at 325° for 20 minutes or until it springs back when touched.

Too little to save, too little to dump, makes the housewife a little bit plump.

Raspberry Streusel Coffee Cake

Marnita Beachy

Filling:

3½ c. unsweetened raspberries	2 Tbsp. lemon juice
1 c. water	1¼ c. sugar
⅔ c. perma-flo	

Batter:

3 c. flour	½ c. butter
1 c. sugar	2 eggs, slightly beaten
1 tsp. baking powder	1 c. sour cream
1 tsp. soda	1 tsp. vanilla

Topping:

½ c. flour	¼ c. butter, softened
½ c. sugar	½ c. chopped pecans

Glaze:

½ c. powdered sugar	½ tsp. vanilla
2 tsp. milk	

Cook raspberries and water for 5 minutes. Add lemon juice. Combine sugar and perma-flo. Stir into fruit mixture. Boil for 2 minutes. Cool. *Batter:* In a bowl combine flour, sugar, baking powder and soda. Cut in butter until mixture resembles coarse crumbs. Stir in eggs, sour cream and vanilla. (Batter will be stiff). Spread half into a 9"x13" greased pan. Spread raspberry filling over batter. Spoon remaining batter over filling. Combine topping ingredients. Sprinkle over top. Bake at 350° for 40–45 minutes or until golden brown. Combine the glaze ingredients; drizzle over warm cake.

Sour Cream Coffee Cake

Raymond & Martha Beachy

Topping:

⅓ c. brown sugar, packed

¼ c. sugar

2 tsp. cinnamon

½ c. chopped pecans

Cake:

½ c. butter, softened

1 c. sugar

2 eggs

1 c. sour cream

1 tsp. vanilla

2 c. flour

1 tsp. baking powder

1 tsp. soda

¼ tsp. salt

Combine topping ingredients; set aside. *Cake:* Cream butter and sugar in a mixing bowl. Add eggs, sour cream and vanilla; mix well. Combine flour, baking powder, soda and salt. Add to creamed mixture; beat until combined. Pour half of batter into a greased 9"x13" pan. Sprinkle with half of topping. Add remaining batter and topping. Bake at 325° for 40 minutes or until cake tests done.

Sour Cream Coconut Cake

Alvin & Charlene Kanagy

1 yellow cake mix

1 tsp. coconut extract

Icing:

8 oz. Cool Whip

1 sm. can sour cream

2 c. powdered sugar

¾ tsp. coconut extract

2 c. coconut

Bake cake according to directions on box; add coconut extract. *Icing:* Mix Cool Whip and sour cream. Beat in powdered sugar and coconut extract. Fold in coconut. Store cake in refrigerator.

Chocolate Chip Sour Cream Cake

Marnita Beachy

3 c. flour
3 tsp. baking powder
1 tsp. soda
1 tsp. salt
1 c. butter
1 c. sugar

3 eggs, well beaten
1 tsp. vanilla
1 c. sour cream
1 pkg. chocolate chips
½ c. brown sugar
1 tsp. cinnamon

Combine flour, baking powder, soda and salt. Cream together butter and white sugar. Add eggs, one at a time beating thoroughly, after each addition. Add vanilla. Add dry ingredients, alternately with sour cream to creamed mixture, ending with dry ingredients. Combine chocolate chips, brown sugar and cinnamon. Spoon half of batter into a greased 9"x13" pan. Sprinkle with ¾ of chocolate mixture and cover with rest of batter and sprinkle with remaining chocolate mixture. Bake at 350° for 30–35 minutes.

The cake is done and ready to remove from oven when it shrinks slightly from the sides of the pan or if it springs back when touched lightly with the finger or if you insert a toothpick and toothpick comes out clean.

Beachy Family Favorites

Sour Cream Chocolate Chip Cake

Alvin & Charlene Kanagy

1 tsp. soda
1 c. sour cream
½ c. margarine
2 eggs
1 c. sugar

2 c. flour
1 tsp. baking powder
pinch of salt
½ tsp. vanilla
1¼ c. chocolate chips

Caramel Frosting:
¾ c. butter
½ c. cream
1½ c. brown sugar

3 c. powdered sugar
1½ tsp. vanilla

Cake: Mix together soda and sour cream; cream margarine, eggs and sugar. Then add flour, baking powder, salt and vanilla. Add to cream mixture and chocolate chips. *Frosting:* Melt butter; remove from heat. Add brown sugar, stirring until smooth. Bring to a boil over low heat. Cool until lukewarm. Add powdered sugar and vanilla. Mix well.

Sour Cream Chocolate Sheet Cake

Melvin & Beth Ann Beachy

2 c. flour

1 tsp. soda

½ c. sour cream

1 tsp. salt

2 c. white sugar

3 eggs, beaten

1 c. butter

1 c. water

4 Tbsp. baking chocolate

Icing:

½ c. butter

⅓ c. milk

1 c. brown sugar

4 Tbsp. baking chocolate

1 c. chopped nuts (optional)

1 c. powdered sugar

1 tsp. vanilla

Cake: Combine flour, soda, sour cream, salt, sugar and beaten eggs in a large bowl. Mix until smooth; set aside. In a small saucepan, combine butter, water and chocolate; bring to a boil. Add chocolate mixture to batter; mix together very well. Batter will be thin. Pour batter into greased 11"x17" jelly-roll pan. Bake at 350° for 25 minutes. Cool in pan on wire rack. *Icing:* Combine butter, milk, brown sugar and chocolate in heavy saucepan. Bring to boil; do not stir. Boil for 3 minutes. Remove from heat; immediately stir in nuts, sugar and vanilla. Pour hot icing onto center of cake; spread gently to outer edges. Cool and enjoy.

Honey Bun Cake
Verna Kay Zook

1 yellow cake mix
¼ c. milk
1 c. butter, softened
4 eggs

1 c. sour cream
⅓ c. brown sugar
⅓ c. chopped pecans
2 tsp. cinnamon

Glaze:
1 c. powdered sugar
1 Tbsp. milk

1 tsp. vanilla

Heat oven to 350°. Grease a 9"x13" pan. Reserve ½ cup dry cake mix. Beat remaining dry cake mix, ¼ cup milk, butter, eggs and sour cream. Spread half the batter in pan. Stir together reserved dry cake mix, brown sugar, pecans and cinnamon; sprinkle over batter in pan. Carefully spread remaining batter evenly over pecan mixture. Bake 40–45 minutes until cake springs back when touched lightly in center. *Glaze:* Stir powdered sugar, milk and vanilla until thin enough to drizzle, adding additional milk if necessary. Poke top of warm cake several times with fork; spread over top of cake.

Hummingbird Cake
Wilmer & Sarah Beachy

3 c. flour, sifted
2 c. sugar
1 tsp. salt
1 tsp. soda
1 tsp. cinnamon
1½ tsp. vanilla

1½ c. vegetable oil
3 eggs, beaten
1½ c. crushed pineapples
1½ c. mashed bananas
1 c. chopped pecans

With a large spoon, mix all dry ingredients. Add vanilla, pineapples, bananas and nuts. Bake in three layer pans at 350° for 30 minutes. Frost with Cream Cheese Icing. Don't beat it when you mix it together.

Mahogany Cake

Raymond & Martha Beachy

2 c. flour
2 c. sugar
2 Tbsp. cocoa, heaping
2½ tsp. soda
½ tsp. salt

2 eggs
⅔ c. sour cream
1 tsp. vanilla
½ c. butter
1 c. boiling water

Filling:
¾ c. cream
1 Tbsp. flour
⅓ c. butter
4 egg yolks

1 c. sugar
1⅓ c. coconut
½ c. pecans

Frosting:
½ c. cocoa
1 tsp. vanilla
3 c. powdered sugar

½ c. butter
6 Tbsp. milk
½ c. chopped nuts

Cake: Mix dry ingredients; add eggs, sour cream, vanilla and melted butter. Mix well; then beat in hot water. Bake in 2 round layer pans at 350° until done about 30 minutes. *Filling:* Combine cream, flour, butter, egg yolks and sugar and cook in saucepan until thick. Stir constantly. Add coconut and nuts. *Frosting:* Combine ingredients and put filling in between layers and on top and frost on sides.

Mississippi Mud Cake

Marnita Beachy

1 c. chopped pecans
1 c. butter
1 (4 oz.) semisweet chocolate
   baking bar, chopped
2 c. sugar
1½ c. flour

¼ c. cocoa
4 lg. eggs
1 tsp. vanilla
¾ tsp. salt
1 (10.5 oz.) bag miniature
   marshmallows

Frosting:
½ c. butter
⅓ c. milk
⅓ c. cocoa

1 lb. powdered sugar
1 tsp. vanilla

Place pecans in single layer in baking sheet. Bake at 350° for 8–10 minutes or until toasted. Melt butter and chocolate, mixing until smooth. Mix next 6 ingredients into chocolate mixture. Pour into a 10"x15" baking sheet and bake at 350° for 20 minutes. Remove from oven and sprinkle evenly with marshmallow. Bake 8–10 minutes more. Drizzle warm cake with frosting and sprinkle evenly with pecans. *Frosting:* Stir together first 3 ingredients over medium heat until butter is melted. Stir constantly and cook until thick (approx. 2 minutes). Remove from heat, beat in powdered sugar and vanilla until smooth.

Oatmeal Cake

Orvan & Marilyn Miller

1¼ c. boiling water
1 c. oatmeal
½ c. margarine
1 c. white sugar
1 c. brown sugar
2 eggs

1 tsp. vanilla
1⅓ c. flour
½ tsp. salt
1 tsp. soda
1 tsp. cinnamon

Topping:
½ c. brown sugar
½ c. chopped nuts
¾ c. coconut

¼ c. butter, melted
3 Tbsp. milk
1 tsp. vanilla

Pour boiling water over oatmeal, let set 20 minutes. Cream together margarine and sugars; add eggs and vanilla. Beat in oatmeal. Sift together flour, cinnamon, soda and salt, put into creamed mixture. Pour into 9"x13" pan and bake at 350° for 35–40 minutes or until done. *Topping:* Melt butter and brown sugar, add rest of ingredients and spread evenly over hot cake. Put cake under broiler and brown approx. 2 minutes. Watch closely! It browns easily.

Orange Juice Cake

Alvin & Charlene Kanagy

4 eggs
½ c. vegetable oil
1 c. orange juice

1 yellow cake mix
¼ c. flour
1 sm. box instant vanilla pudding

Glaze:
1 c. orange juice
½ c. margarine

1 c. sugar

Mix together eggs, vegetable oil, orange juice, cake mix, flour and instant vanilla pudding. Pour into well greased tube pan. Bake at 350° for 45 minutes. *Glaze:* Boil together ingredients and pour over cake within 5 minutes after it is out of oven. Let set approx. 15 minutes; then remove from pan. A very moist cake.

Flattery is like soft soap and soft soap is ninety percent lye!

Peach Upside Down Cake

Raymond & Martha Beachy

Topping:

¼ c. butter
¼ c. honey
1 tsp. cinnamon

¼ tsp. nutmeg
2 c. sliced peaches

Batter:

1 c. whole wheat pastry flour
2 tsp. baking powder
⅓ c. maple syrup
¼ c. vegetable oil

1 egg
3 Tbsp. milk
1 tsp. vanilla
1 tsp. lemon peel, finely grated

Place the butter, honey, cinnamon and nutmeg in a small saucepan. Stir over medium heat until the butter is melted. Pour mixture into bottom of 8" square cake pan. Make an even layer of peaches over the honey-butter mixture. Set the pan aside while you make the batter. Sift together the flour and baking powder. In another bowl, beat together the maple syrup, vegetable oil, egg, milk, vanilla and lemon peel. Stir the flour mixture into the liquid mixture. Beat just enough to mix well; take care not to overmix. Evenly pour the batter over peaches. Bake at 350° for 1 hour or until golden brown.

Peanut Butter Flan Cake

Alvin & Charlene Kanagy

½ pkg. chocolate cake mix

Topping:

3 oz. cream cheese, softened	⅔ c. milk
¼ c. peanut butter	⅓ c. instant vanilla pudding
1½ tsp. white sugar	2¼ c. Cool Whip, divided
½ tsp. vanilla	Reese's peanut butter cups

Prepare cake mix according to package directions, using ½ the ingredients. Pour into a greased flan pan or an 8" square pan. Bake at 350° until toothpick comes out clean. If using a flan pan cool 10 minutes; then invert to a serving plate. *Topping:* Cream together cream cheese and peanut butter; add sugar and vanilla. Whisk milk and pudding, let set until thickened. Fold in peanut butter mixture. Stir in 1½ cup Cool Whip. Spread on cake, top with remaining Cool Whip, cut peanut butter cups into wedges. Set up in whipped topping. Refrigerate.

Yellow Pineapple Cake

Melvin & Beth Ann Beachy

1 yellow cake mix	2 c. milk
2 cans crushed pineapples, drained	8 oz. cream cheese, softened
1 (3½ oz.) box instant vanilla pudding	1¼ c. whipped cream

Bake cake mix according to directions on box. Cool. Drain crushed pineapples, put that on top of cake. Then mix instant vanilla pudding with milk and cream cheese. Put on top of pineapples. Top with whipped cream.

Note: If using raw milk; heat to scalding, then cool to refrigerator cold before mixing with instant pudding.

No Fuss Pumpkin Cake

Melvin & Beth Ann Beachy

2 c. pumpkin, scant

3 eggs

⅓ c. sugar

⅓ c. vegetable oil

1 yellow cake mix

1 Tbsp. pumpkin pie spice

Frosting:

16 oz. vanilla frosting

3 oz. cream cheese, softened

Mix together first 4 ingredients well. Then add cake mix and pumpkin pie spice; mix well again and pour in greased 9"x13" pan and bake at 350° for 25–35 minutes.

Best Ever Strawberry Cake

Marnita Beachy

1 white cake mix

1 box strawberry Jell-O

1 c. vegetable oil

½ c. milk

4 eggs

1 c. fresh or frozen strawberries

Frosting:

1 lb. powdered sugar

½ c. butter

½ c. pecans

½ c. coconut

½ c. strawberries

Blend together cake mix and Jell-O. Add vegetable oil and milk; beat well. Add eggs, one at a time and beat again until eggs are well blended in. Fold in berries. Pour in 9"x13" pan and bake at 350°.

Three-Layer Strawberries and Cream Cake

Renita Faye Helmuth

Cake:

2 c. sugar
1 sm. pkg. strawberry Jell-O
1 c. butter, softened
4 eggs
2¾ c. cake flour

2½ tsp. baking powder
1 c. milk
1 tsp. vanilla
½ c. strawberries, puréed

Filling:

1½ c. heavy whipping cream
2 Tbsp. sugar

½ tsp. vanilla
1½ c. strawberries, sliced

Frosting:

½ c. butter, softened
8 oz. cream cheese, softened
4 c. powdered sugar

2 tsp. vanilla
1½ c. chopped strawberries

In a large bowl, beat sugar, Jell-O and butter until fluffy. Add eggs, one at a time, beating after each. Mix flour and baking powder together and add to sugar mixture in two parts. Alternating with the milk and beating after each addition. Fold in vanilla and strawberries. Divide equally into the three cake pans (9" round cake pans). Bake at 350° for 25 minutes. Cool for 10 minutes, remove cake, and cool completely. *Filling:* Beat whipping cream, sugar and vanilla until stiff. Cover the bottom and middle cake layer each with ⅓ of the whipped cream and ¾ cup sliced strawberries. Set aside remaining whipped cream. *Frosting:* Beat the butter, cream cheese, powdered sugar and vanilla until creamy. Spread frosting around the sides of the cake. Make a pretty piping of frosting along the top edge of the cake. Gently spread remaining whipped cream on cake top. Decorate top with strawberries.

Spice Chiffon Cake

Levi & Katie Beachy

2¼ c. sifted flour
1 tsp. baking powder
¾ tsp. soda
1 tsp. salt
¾ tsp. nutmeg
¾ tsp. cloves
¾ tsp. cinnamon

1 c. brown sugar, packed
⅓ c. vegetable oil
⅔ c. buttermilk, divided
2 egg yolks
2 egg whites
½ c. sugar

Sift together first 7 ingredients into a bowl; then add rest of ingredients. Beat 1 minute; then add another ⅓ cup buttermilk and egg yolks. Beat 1 minute more, then fold in a very stiff meringue of egg whites and sugar. Put in a 9"x13" pan. Bake at 350° for 40–45 minutes.

Turtle Cake

Orvan & Marilyn Miller

1 German chocolate cake mix
14 oz. caramels
½ c. butter or margarine

6 oz. chopped pecans
7 oz. sweetened condensed milk
6 oz. semisweet chocolate chips

Mix cake as on package. Bake half the mix in greased and floured 9"x13" pan at 350° for 15 minutes. In top of double boiler melt together butter, caramels and milk. Remove top of double boiler from heat. Cool mixture slightly and pour over baked half of cake. Pour over the remaining batter. Sprinkle with pecans and chocolate chips. Bake at 350° for 25 minutes.

Wacky Cake

Katrina Beachy

3 c. flour
2 c. sugar
3 Tbsp. cocoa
½ c. vegetable oil
2 c. water

2 tsp. soda
½ tsp. salt
½ tsp. vanilla
2 Tbsp. vinegar

Mix well. Bake at 350° for 45 minutes.

Wacky Cake

Jonathan Lee Miller

3 c. flour
2 c. sugar
4 Tbsp. cocoa
2 tsp. soda
½ tsp. salt

⅔ c. vegetable oil
2 c. water
2 Tbsp. vinegar
2 tsp. vanilla

Mix together dry ingredients, add the rest of the ingredients, and mix well. Bake in a 9"x13" pan at 350° for 45 minutes.

Cool Whip Icing

Melvin & Beth Ann Beachy

1 sm. box instant pudding,
   any kind
¼ c. powdered sugar

1 c. milk
8 oz. Cool Whip

If using raw milk heat until scalding; then cool until refrigerator cold. Then mix with instant pudding. Beat until creamy and add Cool Whip.

Decorator Icing

Marnita Beachy

4 c. powdered sugar
1 c. Crisco
1 tsp. vanilla

4–5 Tbsp. milk or
    to right consistency

Beat everything together.

Frosting For 1 Cake

Melvin & Beth Ann Beachy

½ c. shortening
1 egg
⅓ c. milk
¼ c. cocoa (for chocolate icing)

4 c. powdered sugar
1 tsp. vanilla
¼ tsp. salt

Mix all together until creamy.

Good Creamy Icing

Melvin & Beth Ann Beachy

8 oz. cream cheese
½ c. brown sugar

2 c. Cool Whip
1½ c. powdered sugar

Mix and spread on cake.

Penuche Frosting

Melvin & Beth Ann Beachy

1 c. brown sugar
¼ c. milk
3 Tbsp. butter

1 Tbsp. milk
2 c. powdered sugar (approx.)
1 tsp. vanilla

Cook brown sugar, milk and butter over low heat for 3 minutes. Cool; then add powdered sugar until thick. Add vanilla and milk to desired consistency. Enough for regular size cake. Also good on cinnamon rolls.

To keep icing moist and to prevent cracking, add a pinch of baking soda.

> *If your day is hemmed with
> prayer it is less likely to unravel.*

Cookies & Bars

Fresh Glazed Apple Cookies

Levi & Katie Beachy

½ c. shortening
1⅓ c. sugar
1 egg
1 c. chopped apples
¼ c. milk

2 c. flour
1 tsp. soda
1 tsp. cinnamon
½ tsp. nutmeg
½ tsp. salt

Icing:
1½ c. powdered sugar
1 Tbsp. butter

¼ tsp. vanilla
2 Tbsp. milk

Cream shortening and sugar. Add egg; beat well. Add apples and milk. Mix together dry ingredients. Blend all ingredients together. Bake at 350° for 8–10 minutes or until they spring back when touched lightly. *Icing:* Mix in order given. Frost cookies while still warm.

Butterscotch Dessert Cookies

Melvin & Beth Ann Beachy

1½ c. brown sugar
½ c. margarine
2 eggs
1 tsp. vanilla
2½ c. flour

½ tsp. salt
1 tsp. soda
½ tsp. baking powder
1 c. sour cream

Frosting:
5 Tbsp. butter, browned
1 tsp. vanilla

¼ c. hot water
3 c. powdered sugar, sifted

Cream together sugar and margarine. Add eggs and vanilla, beat until fluffy. Sift together flour, salt, soda and baking powder. Add dry ingredients with sour cream to sugar mixture. Mix thoroughly. Drop by teaspoonfuls on cookie sheet and bake at 400° until done, about 10–12 minutes. *Frosting:* Mix in order given. Frost cookies while still warm.

Chocolate Chip Cookies*

Beachy's Bulk Foods

1 c. margarine	2 eggs
¼ c. white sugar	1 tsp. vanilla
¾ c. brown sugar	2¼ c. flour
1 pkg. or ⅓ c. instant vanilla pudding	1 tsp. soda
	1 c. chocolate chips

Blend first 4 ingredients well. Add eggs and vanilla. Beat well. Mix flour and soda, and add to other mixture along with chocolate chips. Bake at 350° for 8–10 minutes or until they spring back when touched lightly. These cookies usually puff up, then set down some after they are out of the oven. They have a better flavor if not overbaked.

Chocolate Chippers

Lavern Andrew Helmuth

2 c. Crisco	5 c. flour
2 c. sugar	3 tsp. salt
1 c. brown sugar	2 tsp. soda
2 eggs, beaten	4 c. chocolate chips
2 tsp. vanilla	1 c. nuts

Mix Crisco and sugars; add beaten eggs and vanilla. Sift flour, salt and soda; add to sugar mixture. Add chips and nuts. Bake at 375° for 10–15 minutes.

Gluten-Free Chocolate Chip Oatmeal Cookies

Steve & Lorene Helmuth

6 Tbsp. butter	1 tsp. salt
2 c. brown sugar	1–2 tsp. Xanthan Gum
*2 c. flour	1 Tbsp. hot water
3 c. oatmeal	1 tsp. vanilla
1 tsp. soda	2 eggs
1 tsp. baking powder	1 c. chocolate chips

Beat together butter and brown sugar. Mix together flours, oatmeal, soda, salt and baking powder and Xanthan Gum; add to butter mixture. Next add hot water, vanilla and eggs. Mix and add chocolate chips. Dough is usually too dry, you can add 1 cup peanut butter and more hot water. Using vegetable oil instead of butter helps. Flatten cookies. Bake at 350° for 10–15 minutes.

*Note: *Flour consists of: 1 cup rice flour, ½ cup tapioca flour, ½ cup potato flour, mix together before adding to your ingredients.*

Chocolate Chip Oatmeal Cookies

Orvan & Marilyn Miller

1½ c. shortening	4 c. quick oats
2 c. sugar	1 tsp. salt
2 c. brown sugar	2 tsp. soda
4 eggs	1 tsp. baking powder
2 tsp. vanilla	1 pkg. chocolate chips
4 c. flour	nuts, if desired

Mix in order given and drop on greased cookie sheet and bake at 375° until done, about 10–12 minutes.

Note: Reese's peanut butter chips and also other kinds are good instead of chocolate chips.

Outrageous Chocolate Chip Cookies

Matthew David Miller

3 c. sugar
2 c. brown sugar
3 c. butter
3 c. peanut butter
3 tsp. vanilla
6 eggs

6 c. flour
3 c. oatmeal
6 tsp. soda
1½ tsp. salt
chocolate chips

Cream together sugars, butter, and peanut butter. Add vanilla and eggs; beat well. Add rest of ingredients. Bake at 350° for 8–10 minutes or until done.

Chocolate Chip Sandwich Cookies*

Beachy's Bulk Foods

3 c. margarine
2¼ c. brown sugar
¾ c. sugar
6 eggs
3 tsp. vanilla

6 c. flour
3 tsp. soda
1½ c. instant vanilla pudding
1½ c. oatmeal
3 c. chocolate chips

Whoopie Pie Filling:
2 egg whites
1 Tbsp. vanilla

2 c. powdered sugar
1½ c. Crisco

Combine margarine and sugars. Add eggs and vanilla. Stir and add dry ingredients . Bake at 350°. *Filling:* Beat together egg whites and vanilla. Then add powdered sugar and Crisco. Beat well. Continue beating until smooth. Spread on cookie. Place another cookie on top.

Cinnamon Roll Cookies

Melvin & Beth Ann Beachy

1 Tbsp. yeast	2 eggs, beaten
¼ c. warm water	1 c. warm water or scalded milk
1 c. margarine or Crisco	4 c. flour
¾ c. sugar	1 tsp. salt
1 tsp. vanilla	

Sugar Mixture:

¾ c. sugar	1 tsp. cinnamon

Glaze:

⅓ c. butter, slightly browned	1½ tsp. vanilla or maple flavor
2 c. powdered sugar	2–4 Tbsp. hot water

Dissolve yeast in ¼ cup warm water. Cream margarine or Crisco and ¾ cup sugar. Add vanilla, eggs and 1 cup warm water or scalded milk. Mix in yeast, flour and salt. Refrigerate overnight. You may need a little more flour before making rolls. Divide dough in half and roll each in an 12"x18" rectangle. Sprinkle with sugar mixture. Roll up tightly. Cut into ½" wide slices; put on cookie sheet; press flat with hand. Bake at 375° for 12 minutes. Cool and glaze.

Coconut Oatmeal Cookies

Gary Lynn Helmuth

4 c. shortening	7 c. flour
4 c. brown sugar	4 tsp. soda
4 c. sugar	4 tsp. baking powder
8 eggs	4 tsp. vanilla
10 c. oatmeal	2 c. nuts
2–4 c. coconut	2 pkg. chocolate chips

Mix together. Chill dough for several hours. Bake at 350°. Do not overbake.

Little Debbie Cookies*

Beachy's Bulk Foods

6 c. butter	11 c. flour
12 c. brown sugar	6 tsp. soda
16 eggs	4 tsp. salt
2 tsp. vanilla	8 tsp. cinnamon
16 c. quick oats	2 tsp. nutmeg

Icing:

2 egg whites	2 c. powdered sugar
1 Tbsp. vanilla	1½ c. Crisco

Cream together butter and sugar. Add eggs and vanilla; beat well. Add dry ingredients. Bake at 350° for 10 minutes. *Icing:* Beat egg whites and vanilla together until soft peaks form. Add powdered sugar and Crisco; beat well until smooth. Spread on cookies and top with another cookie.

Little Debbie Cookies

Steven & Lorene Helmuth

1 c. margarine	1½ tsp. nutmeg
3 c. brown sugar	1 tsp. soda
4 eggs	3 c. flour
2 tsp. cinnamon	3 c. oatmeal

Filling:

2 egg whites	4 c. powdered sugar
2 tsp. vanilla	1 c. Crisco
¼ c. milk	

Cream margarine, sugar, eggs and spices. Add rest of ingredients and roll into small balls. Flatten on a cookie sheet. Bake at 350°. Put filling between 2 cookies.

Holstein Cookies

Marcia Kay Miller

½ c. margarine
¼ c. sugar
¾ c. brown sugar
1 tsp. soda
1 tsp. vanilla
2 eggs

2½ c. flour
8 oz. chocolate chips
1 (3 oz.) box vanilla instant
    pudding
1 (3 oz.) box chocolate instant
    pudding

To make 2 color cookies make 1 batch with vanilla and 1 batch with chocolate pudding. Take a little of each dough and roll together, then roll in white sugar before baking. Flatten on cookie sheet. Bake at 350°. Do not overbake.

Honey Cakes

Lamar Jay Miller

¼ c. butter
¾ c. honey
1 egg
2 c. whole wheat flour

2 tsp. salt
2 tsp. baking powder
2 Tbsp. milk
1 tsp. vanilla

Cream butter; add honey and beaten egg and beat until fluffy. In a separate bowl; mix flour, salt, vanilla and baking powder. Add dry ingredients alternately with milk and vanilla to creamed mixture. Mix thoroughly. Drop by teaspoonfuls onto greased sheets 2–3" apart. Bake at 350° for 5–7 minutes.

Lemon Puff Cookies

Melvin & Beth Ann Beachy

2 eggs
1 c. sugar
½ c. shortening
½ c. margarine
2 tsp. lemon extract

2¼ c. Tbsp. flour
½ tsp. baking powder
½ tsp. soda
½ tsp. salt

Beat eggs until very light. Add sugar and continue to beat. Add softened shortening, margarine, lemon extract and dry ingredients; mix well. Allow to stay in refrigerator several hours before baking. Make into little balls and roll in powdered sugar before baking. Bake at 375°.

Monster Cookies*

Beachy's Bulk Foods

4 c. brown sugar
4 c. sugar
1 lb. margarine
12 eggs
1 Tbsp. vanilla
1 Tbsp. light corn syrup

4½ c. peanut butter
9 c. oatmeal
9 c. flour
8 tsp. soda
1 lb. chocolate chips
1 lb. M&M's

Cream together sugars and margarine. Beat in eggs, vanilla, syrup and peanut butter. Add oatmeal, flour, soda and chocolate chips. Drop on cookie sheets and press in 3 M&M's on each cookie. Bake at 350° for 10 minutes. Makes approx. 20 dozen.

Oatmeal Butterscotch Cookies

Kevin Zook

1 c. butter	1 tsp. soda
½ c. raw sugar	½ tsp. salt
½ c. brown sugar	½ tsp. cinnamon
2 eggs	3 c. rolled oats
1 tsp. vanilla	1½ c. butterscotch chips
1¼ c. flour	

Beat butter and sugars; add eggs and vanilla. Add rest of ingredients; mix well. Bake on ungreased cookie sheet at 375°. Bake 7–8 minutes for a chewy cookie or 9–10 minutes for a crisp cookie.

Oatmeal Chocolate Chip Cookies*

Beachy's Bulk Foods

4 c. shortening (3¼ c. if butter and lard are used)	6 c. flour
2⅔ c. brown sugar	4 tsp. soda
3 c. sugar	1 Tbsp. salt
8 eggs (add 1 at a time)	4 c. nuts or coconut
¼ c. hot water	4 c. chocolate chips
¼ c. vanilla	8 c. quick-cooking oats
	1 c. instant pudding

Sift flour, soda and salt together. Mix in order given in a very large bowl. Drop by teaspoonfuls on a greased baking sheet. Bake in oven at about 350°–375°. Makes about 250 medium-sized cookies. This recipe may be cut in half.

Chewy Oat Cookies

Orvan & Marilyn Miller

⅔ c. butter or margarine
1 c. brown sugar, packed
⅓ c. peanut butter
1 tsp. vanilla
2 eggs
1 c. flour
½ tsp. soda
½ tsp. baking powder
¼ tsp. salt
½ c. buttermilk or sour milk
2 c. quick or rolled oats
1 c. oat bran
1 c. sunflower seeds
1 c. raisins
1 c. chocolate chips

Beat together butter, brown sugar and peanut butter until fluffy. Beat in vanilla, eggs and buttermilk. Add rest of ingredients. Drop on greased baking sheet and flatten slightly. Bake at 375° for around 10 minutes or until golden brown. Yield: 60 cookies.

Oatmeal Chocolate Chip Cookies

Kevin Zook

1 c. shortening
1 c. butter
1 c. brown sugar
1 c. raw sugar
4 eggs, beaten
2 tsp. hot water
2 tsp. vanilla
3½ c. flour
2 tsp. soda
1 tsp. salt
3½ c. rolled oats
3 c. chocolate chips

Beat together shortening, butter and sugars. Add eggs, hot water and vanilla. Beat well. Add all ingredients in order given. Bake at 350° until light brown.

Oatmeal Raisin Cookies*

Beachy's Bulk Foods

1 c. margarine	2 eggs
¼ c. sugar	1 c. raisins
¾ c. brown sugar	2½ c. quick oats
1 pkg. vanilla instant pudding	1¾ c. flour
(or ⅓ cup)	1 tsp. soda

Combine margarine, sugars and instant pudding. Stir until smooth and creamy. Add eggs; beat well. Add quick oats and raisins. Stir well. Add flour and soda, stir. Drop on cookie sheets and bake at 350° for 8–10 minutes.

Orange Candy Cookies

Melvin & Beth Ann Beachy

1 lb. orange slice candy	1 tsp. vanilla
¼ c. flour	1¾ c. flour
1 c. butter	1 tsp. baking powder
1 c. brown sugar	¼ tsp. salt
2 c. quick oats	1 tsp. soda
1 c. sugar	1 c. coconut
2 eggs	

Cut orange slices into small pieces. Mix candy with ¼ cup flour. Cream butter and sugar; add eggs and vanilla and beat very well. Sift together dry ingredients 2 or 3 times; then add to creamed mixture. Stir in quick oats, coconut and candy mixture. Drop by teaspoonfuls on greased cookie sheet. Bake at 375° for 10–15 or until light brown. Do not overbake!

Peanut Butter Cookies

Larry Allen Miller

1 c. margarine	1 tsp. vanilla
1 c. peanut butter	2 tsp. soda
1 c. sugar	¼ tsp. salt
1 c. brown sugar	3 c. flour
3 eggs	

In a mixing bowl, cream margarine, peanut butter and sugars. Add eggs one at a time; beat well after each one. Add vanilla, then dry ingredients. Roll into about 1½" balls, flatten with a fork. Bake at 375° for 10–15 minutes.

Peanut Butter Chocolate Chip Cookies

Abner & Sovilla Mae Zook

1½ c. butter	4 tsp. vanilla
1½ c. brown sugar	5 c. flour
1 c. raw sugar	2 tsp. soda
1 c. peanut butter	½ tsp. salt
4 eggs	2 c. chocolate chips

Beat butter and sugars together. Add peanut butter; beat well. Add eggs and vanilla; beat well. Mix in flour, soda and salt. Stir in chocolate chips. Bake at 350° on ungreased baking sheets until light brown.

Peanut Butter Chocolate Chip Cookies

Jonathan Lee Miller

¾ c. peanut butter
½ c. butter, softened
½ c. sugar
½ c. brown sugar, packed
½ tsp. vanilla
1 egg
5 Tbsp. milk

1¼ c. flour
¾ tsp. soda
½ tsp. baking powder
¼ tsp. salt
1 c. chocolate chips
½ c. peanuts (optional)

In a bowl, combine peanut butter, butter, sugars and vanilla. Beat until creamy. Beat in egg and milk. First dissolve soda in milk. Add flour, soda, baking powder, salt and chocolate chips. Mix together and drop on cookie sheets. Bake at 350° for 10–12 minutes.

Peanut Butter Temptations (cookies or bars)

Steven & Lorene Helmuth

1 c. peanut butter
1 c. margarine
¾ c. sugar
1 c. brown sugar
2 eggs

2¾ c. flour
¾ tsp. soda
¾ tsp. baking powder
¾ tsp. salt
1 tsp. vanilla

Cream butters and sugars. Add eggs. Add rest of ingredients and mix well. Drop on cookie sheet and press down with a fork and bake until done. Press all the dough into a cookie sheet if you want bars.

Peanut Butter Oaties

Larry Allen Miller

½ c. butter or margarine
½ c. peanut butter
½ c. brown sugar
¼ c. sugar
1 egg
1 tsp. vanilla

1¼ c. quick oats
½ c. flour
1 tsp. soda
1 c. chocolate chips
nuts (optional)
coconut (optional)

Mix in order given. Bake at 350° for 10–11 minutes.

Pumpkin Cookies

Melvin & Beth Ann Beachy

2 c. shortening
2 c. brown sugar
2 eggs
2 c. pumpkin
4 c. flour
2 tsp. baking powder

2 tsp. soda
1 tsp. salt
1 tsp. nutmeg
5 tsp. cinnamon
½ tsp. ginger

Never Fail Icing:
½ c. margarine
1 c. brown sugar
¼ c. cream or rich milk

vanilla
maple flavor
powdered sugar

Bake at 350° for 10–20 minutes. *Icing:* Melt margarine in saucepan; add brown sugar and cream or rich milk; boil together 3 minutes. Add vanilla, maple flavor and powdered sugar.

Rice Krispie Cookies

Orvan & Marilyn Miller

1 c. margarine
1 c. brown sugar
1 c. sugar
½ c. peanut butter
1 tsp. vanilla
2 eggs
1 c. oatmeal
3 c. Rice Krispies

2 c. flour
1 tsp. soda
½ tsp. baking powder
½ tsp. salt
½ c. peanut butter or
    butterscotch chips
½ c. nuts (optional)

Mix well. Bake at 350° for 10–15 minutes.

Sour Cream Cut-Outs

Treva Kay Beachy

1 c. butter, softened
1½ c. sugar
3 eggs
1 c. sour cream

2 tsp. lemon flavor or vanilla
3½ c. flour
2 tsp. baking powder
1 tsp. soda

Frosting:
⅓ c. butter, softened
2 c. powdered sugar
2–3 Tbsp. milk

1½ tsp. vanilla
¼ tsp. salt

In a mixing bowl, cream butter and sugar. Beat in eggs. Add sour cream and vanilla; mix well. Combine flour, baking powder and soda; add to the creamed mixture and mix well. Chill dough at least 2 hours or overnight. Roll out on a heavily floured board to ¼" thickness. Cut with cookie cutter. Place on lightly greased cookie sheets. Bake at 350° for 10–12 minutes or until cookie springs back when lightly touched. Do not overbake. Cool. Mix all frosting ingredients until smooth; spread on cookies.

Snickerdoodles*

Beachy's Bulk Foods

1 c. margarine
1½ c. sugar
2 eggs
2¾ c. flour

1 tsp. soda
½ tsp. salt
2 tsp. cream of tartar

Mix together shortening and sugar; add eggs and beat well. Mix flour, soda, salt and cream of tartar. Add to shortening mixture. Chill dough. Roll into balls the size of small walnuts. Roll in a mixture of 2 teaspoon cinnamon and 2 tablespoons sugar. Place 2" apart on cookie sheet. Bake until lightly browned but still soft. These cookies puff up at first, then flatten out with crinkled tops. Bake at 400° for 8–10 minutes.

Sorghum Cookies

Levi & Katie Beachy

Small Batch:	Large Batch:
1½ c. margarine	6 c.
2½ c. sugar	10 c.
2 eggs	8 eggs
½ c. buttermilk	2 c.
½ c. sorghum or molasses	2 c.
1 tsp. baking powder	4 tsp.
2 tsp. cinnamon	8 tsp.
5½ c. flour	22 c.
4 tsp. soda	16 tsp.

Cream shortening and sugar. Dissolve soda in buttermilk. Add eggs, buttermilk and sorghum. Add the rest of dry ingredients. Chill dough, then roll into small balls. Dip in sugar. Bake at 350° for 10–15 minutes. Do not store these cookies in a cool place as they will get hard. Room temperature is best.

Christmas Sugar Cookies

Raymond & Martha Beachy

1 c. butter	½ tsp. soda
1 c. sugar	1 tsp. cream of tartar
2 eggs	½ tsp. baking powder
1 tsp. vanilla	3 c. flour
¾ tsp. salt	

Cream butter and sugar. Beat in eggs and vanilla. Gradually add dry ingredients. May need to add more flour. Roll on a heavily floured surface and cut with cookie cutter. Bake at 375° for 8–10 minutes.

Sugar Cookies*

Beachy's Bulk Foods

3 c. margarine	1 Tbsp. lemon flavoring
5 c. sugar	1 Tbsp. soda
4 eggs	2 Tbsp. baking powder
3 c. sweet milk	½ tsp. salt
2 Tbsp. vanilla	10 c. flour

Cream margarine and sugar together. Add eggs and stir well. Then add milk, vanilla and lemon flavoring. Sift soda and baking powder with salt and flour. Add to the other ingredients. Drop on sheets by teaspoonfuls or cookie dipper. Sprinkle with colored sugars. Bake at 375° for 8 minutes or until they spring back when touched lightly.

Toll House Oatmeal Cookies

Raymond & Martha Beachy

1½ c. flour	1 c. butter, melted
1 tsp. soda	¾ c. brown sugar
2 c. oatmeal	¾ c. sugar
1 c. nuts (optional)	2 eggs, beaten
2 c. chocolate chips	1 tsp. hot water
1 tsp. vanilla	1 tsp. salt

Mix the first 5 ingredients together. Mix the rest of the ingredients together and dissolve. Add to the dry ingredients and mix well. Drop by teaspoonfuls on cookie sheet and bake at 350° for 10–15 minutes. Do not overbake.

Walnut Frosties

Raymond & Martha Beachy

½ c. margarine	2 c. flour
1 c. brown sugar	½ tsp. soda
1 egg	¼ tsp. salt
1 tsp. vanilla	

Topping:

1 c. chopped walnuts	¼ c. sour cream
½ c. brown sugar	

Combine margarine, brown sugar, egg and vanilla. Beat until light and fluffy. Sift flour, salt and soda together. Gradually add to sugar mixture. Shape dough into 1" balls. Place on ungreased cookie sheet. Make a depression in the center of each cookie. *Topping:* Mix together. Fill each cookie depression with 1 teaspoon topping. Bake at 350° for 10 minutes.

Whoopie Pies

Robert & Dorothy Beachy, Willard & Carol Ann Helmuth

3 c. vegetable oil
6 c. sugar
1½ c. cocoa
8 eggs
2 Tbsp. soda

3 c. buttermilk
2 Tbsp. salt
3 c. hot water
12 c. flour

Filling:
6 egg whites
2 Tbsp. vanilla
3 c. shortening

2 Tbsp. water
powdered sugar

Mix ingredients together and bake at 375°. *Filling:* Beat egg whites until stiff; add shortening, vanilla, water and powdered sugar until desired consistency. Yield: 8 dozen.

Pumpkin Whoopie Pies*

Beachy's Bulk Foods

4 c. brown sugar
2 c. vegetable oil
4 eggs
1½ c. pumpkin
1½ c. water
2 tsp. vanilla
6 c. flour

2 tsp. salt
2 tsp. baking powder
2 tsp. soda
2 tsp. cinnamon
1 tsp. ginger
½ tsp. cloves

Mix brown sugar and vegetable oil together, then beat in eggs. Add pumpkin, water and vanilla. Stir; then add the dry ingredients. Mix well. Frost with Whoopie Pie Frosting. Top with another cookie.

Whoopie Pies*

Beachy's Bulk Foods

1 c. shortening
  (we like to use lard)
2 c. sugar
2 eggs
2 tsp. vanilla
½ tsp. salt

1 c. thick sour milk or buttermilk
1 c. cold water
4 c. flour
2 tsp. soda
1 c. cocoa

Whoopie Pie Filling:
2 egg whites
1 Tbsp. vanilla

2 c. powdered sugar
1½ c. Crisco

Cream together shortening and sugar; then add eggs, vanilla and salt; beat well. Then add sour milk or buttermilk and cold water. Stir well. Mix together then add flour, soda and cocoa. May need to add some more flour if milk is not thick. Bake at 350° for 8 minutes or until springs back when touched lightly. *Filling:* Beat together egg whites and vanilla. Then add powdered sugar and Crisco. Beat well, and continue beating until smooth. Spread this on cookie. Place another cookie on top.

When making chocolate chip cookies: use only ¾ of the butter the recipe calls for. Instead of flat, oily cookies you get thick, chewy cookies.

Strawberries and Cream Filling for Sandwich Style Cookies

Steve & Lorene Helmuth

2 egg whites	¾ c. Crisco
2 Tbsp. vanilla	powdered sugar
4 tsp. flour	½ c. chopped strawberries, drained
4 tsp. milk	well or put through sieve

Beat egg white until stiff; then add rest of ingredients adding enough powdered sugar until you have desired consistency. Spread on back side of one cookie and top with another to make a sandwich. Filling can be piped on with a wide decorator's frosting tip for a special occasion.

$250 Cookies

Orvan & Marilyn Miller

2 c. butter	24 oz. chocolate chips
2 c. brown sugar	1 tsp. salt
2 c. sugar	2 tsp. soda
4 eggs	2 tsp. baking powder
2 tsp. vanilla	4 c. flour
5 c. oatmeal	3 c. nuts
1 (8 oz.) Hershey bar	

Cream butter and sugars. Add eggs and vanilla. Add rest of ingredients and roll into balls and place on cookie sheets 2" apart. Bake at 375° for 8–10 minutes.

Banana Nut Bars*

Beachy's Bulk Foods

2 c. Crisco	3¾ tsp. baking powder
5 c. sugar	3¾ tsp. soda
9 eggs	1 Tbsp. salt
3¾ c. mashed bananas	7½ c. flour
2 c. nuts	2 c. buttermilk

If buttermilk is not available use 2 cups water and ½ c. buttermilk powder.

Basic Brownies

Jeremy Allen Helmuth

1½ c. flour	1 c. vegetable oil
2 c. sugar	4 eggs
½ c. cocoa	1 Tbsp. vanilla
½ tsp. salt	½ c. chopped walnuts (optional)

In a mixing bowl, combine flour, sugar, cocoa, salt, vegetable oil, eggs, vanilla and nuts. Stir vigorously for 3 minutes until batter is well blended and creamy. Pour into 9"x13" cake pan. Bake at 350° for 30–35 minutes.

Busy Day Brownies

Raymond & Martha Beachy

2¼ c. flour	1½ c. shortening
3 c. sugar	6 eggs
1 c. cocoa	3 tsp. vanilla
1½ tsp. salt	1½ c. nuts (optional)

Place all ingredients in mixing bowl, and stir until well blended. Spread in a large greased bar pan. Bake at 350° for 30 minutes. Cool and cut. Enjoy!

Cream Cheese Brownies

Willard & Carol Ann Helmuth

chocolate cake mix	1 egg
8 oz. cream cheese	½ c. sugar

Mix cake mix according to directions. Put in a 11"x17" cookie sheet with sides. Beat well cream cheese, egg and white sugar; then drop by tablespoon on top of cake and swirl with fork for marble effect. Sprinkle with chocolate chips. Bake at 350° for approx. 22–25 minutes. Do not overbake.

Butterscotch Pecan Bars

Abner & Sovilla Mae Zook

1 c. flour	2 c. brown sugar
2 tsp. baking powder	2 eggs
½ tsp. salt	2 tsp. vanilla
½ c. butter	1 c. chopped pecans

Mix flour, baking powder and salt. Melt butter; remove from heat. Add brown sugar and eggs. Add dry ingredients; mix thoroughly. Add vanilla and nuts; mix. Put into a greased 9"x9" pan. Bake at 375° for 30 minutes. Cut into squares when cold.

Can't Leave Alone Bars

Melvin & Beth Ann Beachy

1 yellow cake mix	½ c. butter
2 eggs	1 c. chocolate chips
⅓ c. vegetable oil	1 can sweetened condensed milk

Mix cake mix, eggs and vegetable oil. Press into bottom of a 9"x13" pan, reserving ¾ cup for the top. Melt butter, chocolate chips and sweetened condensed milk. Pour over crust. Put small dabs of reserved crust over top. Bake at 350° for 35–40 minutes.

Cappuccino Bars

Raymond & Martha Beachy

1¼ c. sugar
1 c. butter
2 eggs
¼ c. syrup
1 tsp. vanilla
1 tsp. rum extract

½ tsp. salt
3 c. flour
2 Tbsp. instant coffee
¾ tsp. baking powder
½ tsp. soda
1 c. chocolate chips

Heat oven to 350°. Beat together butter and sugar. Add eggs, syrup, vanilla and rum extract. Beat until light and fluffy. Mix dry ingredients. Add to creamed mixture and mix until well blended. Spread on bottom of 9"x13" greased and floured pan. Sprinkle with chocolate chips. Bake 30–35 minutes.

Caramel Toffee Bars

Abner & Sovilla Mae Zook

2½ c. cake flour
½ c. sugar
2 c. margarine, divided
1 c. brown sugar
¼ c. corn syrup

1 can sweetened condensed milk
1 tsp. vanilla
2 Tbsp. butter
2 c. chocolate chips

Combine flour, sugar and 1 cup margarine until crumbly. Press into 12"x15" pan. Bake at 350° for approx. 20 minutes. Bring brown sugar, 1 cup margarine, corn syrup and condensed milk to a boil over low heat and boil for 5 minutes, stirring carefully. Remove from heat. Add vanilla. Cool for 10 minutes. Pour over baked crust. Melt butter and chocolate chips together in saucepan. Pour over second layer.

Chocolate Chip Bars

Matthew David Miller
Brandon Beachy

½ c. sugar
⅓ c. brown sugar
½ c. margarine or butter,
  softened
1 tsp. vanilla
1 egg

1¼ c. flour
½ tsp. soda
¼ tsp. salt
6 oz. chocolate chips
½ c. nuts (optional)

Heat oven to 375°. Mix sugars, margarine or butter and vanilla. Beat in egg. Stir in flour, soda and salt. Mix in nuts and chocolate chips. Spread dough in 9"x13" pan. Bake 12–14 minutes, or until light brown.

Chocolate Chip Bars

Abner & Sovilla Mae Zook
Katrina Beachy

2 eggs
1½ c. brown sugar
⅔ c. vegetable oil
1 tsp. vanilla

1½ c. flour
1½ tsp. baking powder
½ tsp. salt
¾ c. chocolate chips

Beat eggs until thick and foamy. Add sugar; beat well. Add vegetable oil and vanilla; beat well. Add flour, baking powder and salt. Fold in chocolate chips. Variation: Use butterscotch chips instead of chocolate chips.

Chocolate Chip Cheesecake Bars

Wilmer & Sarah Beachy

¾ c. shortening	1½ c. flour
¾ c. sugar	1 tsp. salt
⅓ c. brown sugar	¾ tsp. soda
1½ tsp. vanilla	1½ c. miniature chocolate chips
1 egg	

Filling:

16 oz. cream cheese, softened	¾ c. sugar
2 eggs	1 tsp. vanilla

Set aside ⅓ of dough for topping. Press remaining dough in 9"x13" pan. Bake at 350° for 8 minutes. Spoon filling over crust. Drop reserved dough over filling. Bake at 350° for 35–40 minutes.

Davy Crockett Bars

Lamar Jay Miller

1 c. sugar	1 tsp. baking powder
1 c. brown sugar	½ tsp. salt
1 c. shortening	2 c. flour
3 eggs	2 c. quick oats
1 tsp. maple flavoring	1 c. nuts or chocolate chips
1 tsp. soda	

Mix ingredients in order given. Bake at 350° for 40–45 minutes.

Deluxe Chocolate Marshmallow Bars

Melvin & Beth Ann Beachy

¾ c. margarine
1½ c. sugar
3 eggs
1 tsp. vanilla
1⅓ c. flour

½ tsp. baking powder
½ tsp. salt
3 Tbsp. baking cocoa
4 c. miniature marshmallows
½ c. chopped nuts (optional)

Topping:
1⅓ c. chocolate chips
3 Tbsp. butter or margarine

1 c. peanut butter
2 c. Rice Krispie cereal

In a mixing bowl, cream butter and sugar. Add eggs and vanilla; beat until fluffy. Combine flour, baking powder, salt and cocoa; add to creamed mixture. Stir in nuts, if desired. Spread in a greased jelly-roll pan. Bake at 350° for 15–18 minutes. Sprinkle marshmallows evenly over cake; return to oven for 2–3 minutes. Using a knife dipped in water, spread the melted marshmallows evenly over cake. Cool. *Topping:* Combine chocolate chips, butter and peanut butter in a small saucepan. Cook over low heat, stirring constantly until melted and well blended. Remove from heat; stir in cereal. Spread over bars. Chill.

To keep cookies soft, place a slice of bread in the cookie container with the cookies.

Fudge Nut Bars

Alvin & Charlene Kanagy

1 c. margarine	2½ c. flour
2 c. brown sugar	1 tsp. soda
2 eggs	1 tsp. salt
2 tsp. vanilla	2 c. oatmeal

Filling:

1 can sweetened condensed milk	2 tsp. vanilla
2 Tbsp. margarine	2 c. chocolate chips
½ tsp. salt	

Cream together margarine and sugar until fluffy. Beat in eggs and vanilla. Add flour, soda, salt and oatmeal. Mix well. *Filling:* Combine condensed milk, margarine, salt, vanilla and chocolate chips; heat until melted. Reserve 1 cup dough; press rest of dough in bottom of cookie sheet, pour chocolate mixture on top; then drop reserved dough on top of chocolate. Bake at 350° for 40–45 minutes.

No Bake Granola Bars

Lamar Jay Miller

½ c. brown sugar	½ c. chocolate chips
½ c. corn syrup	1 c. raisins
1 c. peanut butter	½ c. coconut
1 tsp. vanilla	½ c. sunflower seeds
1½ c. quick oats	2 Tbsp. sesame seeds (optional)
1½ c. Rice Krispies	

In medium saucepan, combine brown sugar and syrup. Bring to a boil, stirring constantly. Remove from heat. Stir in peanut butter and vanilla. Blend well. Pour over rest of ingredients; mix well. Press into 9"x13" pan. Cool; cut into bars.

Granola Bars

Brandon Beachy

1 lb. marshmallows	8 c. Rice Krispies
¼ c. margarine	4 c. oatmeal
¼ c. vegetable oil	1 c. coconut
¼ c. peanut butter	1 c. chocolate chips
½ c. honey	1 c. graham cracker crumbs

Melt together first 5 ingredients. Mix in rest of ingredients and mix well. Press on cookie sheets, then cut into bars.

Meringue Coconut Brownies

Alvin & Charlene Kanagy

¾ c. butter, softened	1 tsp. baking powder
½ c. brown sugar, divided	¼ tsp. soda
½ c. sugar	¼ tsp. salt
3 egg yolks	2 c. chocolate chips
1 tsp. vanilla	1 c. coconut
2 c. flour	¾ c. chopped walnuts

Meringue:

3 egg whites	1 c. brown sugar

In a large mixing bowl, cream butter and sugars. Add egg yolks and vanilla. Beat 2 minutes. Combine flour, baking powder, soda and salt; add to creamed mixture. Mix well (batter will be thick). Spread in a greased 9"x13" pan. Sprinkle with chocolate chips, coconut and walnuts. *Meringue:* Beat egg whites until soft peaks form. Add brown sugar. Beat until stiff peaks form. Spread over top. Bake at 350° for 30–35 minutes or until toothpick comes out clean. Store in refrigerator. Yield: 3–3½ dozen.

Monster Cookie Bars

Anna Viola Beachy

½ c. margarine or butter, melted	1 tsp. Karo
1½ c. creamy peanut butter	4 c. oatmeal
1 c. sugar	2 tsp. soda
1¼ c. brown sugar	1 c. M&M's
3 eggs	¾ c. chocolate chips

Heat oven to 350°. Mix all the ingredients in the order given. I put it in a jelly-roll size pan, but if you prefer thicker bars, put in a 9"x13". Bake for 15–20 minutes. Do not overbake. Slightly underbaked are best!

Mounds Bars

Merlyn Jay Helmuth

1st Layer:

2 c. crushed graham crackers	½ c. sugar
½ c. melted butter	

2nd Layer:

4 c. flaked coconut	2 cans sweetened condensed milk

3rd Layer:

24 oz. chocolate chips	¼ c. peanut butter

Bake crust at 350° for 10 minutes. *2nd Layer:* Mix and spread on crust; bake another 15 minutes. *3rd Layer:* Spread on 2nd layer while still hot. Chill. Cut into small squares.

Peanut Butter Brownies

Melvin & Beth Ann Beachy

6 eggs	1 Tbsp. vanilla
3 c. sugar	1½ Tbsp. baking powder
1½ c. brown sugar	1½ tsp. salt
1 c. peanut butter	½ c. chopped peanuts
½ c. margarine	4 c. flour

Combine eggs, sugars, peanut butter, margarine and vanilla and blend well. Add dry ingredients, mix only until mixture is smooth. Put in lightly greased pans. Bake at 350° for 25 minutes.

Peanut Butter Fingers

JoAnna Sue Miller

½ c. margarine or butter	½ tsp. soda
½ c. sugar	½ tsp. vanilla
½ c. brown sugar	1 c. flour
1 egg	1 c. quick oats
⅓ c. peanut butter	1 c. chocolate chips
¼ tsp. salt	

Frosting:

½ c. powdered sugar	2–4 Tbsp. milk
¼ c. peanut butter	

Mix together first 3 ingredients; then add egg, peanut butter, salt, soda and vanilla; blend and add flour and quick oats. Spread in 9"x13" pan. Bake at 350° for 20 minutes. Don't overbake! As soon as you take it out of the oven, sprinkle with 1 cup chocolate chips. *Frosting:* Mix together powdered sugar, peanut butter and milk. Drizzle this mixture over top. Let set a bit, then swirl with spoon.

No Bake Peanut Butter Bars

Raymond & Martha Beachy

1 pkg. crushed graham crackers
4 c. powdered sugar
1 c. peanut butter

1 c. butter, melted
1 (12 oz.) pkg. chocolate chips

Combine all ingredients except chocolate chips. Press into a 9"x13" pan. Melt chocolate chips; spread evenly over bars.

Pumpkin Bars*

Beachy's Bulk Foods

2 c. sugar
1 c. vegetable oil
4 eggs
2 c. pumpkin
2 c. flour

2 tsp. cinnamon
½ tsp. salt
2 tsp. baking powder
1 tsp. soda

Frosting:
3 oz. cream cheese
6 Tbsp. margarine
1 Tbsp. cream or milk

1 tsp. vanilla
2 c. powdered sugar

Mix together sugar and vegetable oil. Add eggs and beat well; add pumpkin and stir. Mix together rest of ingredients. Gradually add to pumpkin mixture. Bake at 350° for 20–25 minutes, or if you insert a toothpick, it comes out clean. *Frosting:* Cream together ingredients, gradually add powdered sugar. Spread on bars.

Pumpkin Roll*

Beachy's Bulk Foods

3 eggs
1 c. sugar
⅔ c. pumpkin
1 tsp. lemon juice
1 tsp. baking powder

¾ c. flour
2 tsp. cinnamon
1 tsp. ginger
½ tsp. nutmeg
½ tsp. salt

Filling:
6 oz. cream cheese
1 c. powdered sugar

¼ c. butter
½ tsp. vanilla

Beat eggs on high speed for 5 minutes. Beat in sugar, pumpkin, and lemon juice. Add the dry ingredients. Mix well and spread into a well-greased and floured 10"x15" pan. Top with 1 cup chopped walnuts. Bake at 375° until done. Turn out on towel sprinkled with powdered sugar. Roll lengthwise and let cool completely while still rolled. *Filling:* Beat well. When pumpkin roll is completely cool, unroll and spread on filling. Reroll and chill.

Formica Tops: Polish them to a sparkle with club soda.

Sour Cream Raisin Bars

Wesley & Martha Beachy

1 c. brown sugar	1 tsp. soda
1 c. butter, softened	1¾ c. oatmeal
1¾ c. flour	

Filling:

2 c. raisins	1 c. sugar
¾ c. water	3 Tbsp. cornstarch
3 egg yolks	1 Tbsp. vanilla
1½ c. sour cream	

Cream sugar and butter. Mix flour, soda and oatmeal; add to sugar and butter mixture. Put half of crumbs into a 9"x13" pan. Bake at 325° for 7 minutes. *Filling:* Cook raisins in water for 10 minutes. Drain and cool; set aside. Mix egg yolks, sour cream, sugar and cornstarch. Cook on medium heat, stirring constantly until boiling and thickened. Add raisins and vanilla. Pour over baked crust, top with remaining crumbs. Bake at 300° for an additional 30 minutes.

Twinkie Filling

Melvin & Beth Ann Beachy

5 Tbsp. flour	1 tsp. vanilla
1 c. milk	½ c. butter
1 c. sugar	½ c. Crisco
½ tsp. salt	

Mix flour with milk and cook until thick, cool. Then beat until fluffy. Add other ingredients beating well as you add each one.

Note: Put this between two sheet cakes of your choice of flavor.

Candy

Cashew Crunch

Melvin & Beth Ann Beachy

1 c. margarine (Blue Bonnet)   1½ c. cashews or peanuts
1 c. sugar

   Melt margarine in heavy skillet, stir in sugar and add cashews or peanuts. Cook, stirring constantly until mixture is golden brown and peanuts begin to pop, about 12–14 minutes. Spread in jelly-roll pan and let cool.

Twix Candy Bars

Robert & Dorothy Beachy

½ c. sugar   1 c. crushed graham crackers
½ c. brown sugar   ¾ c. peanut butter
½ c. butter   1 c. chocolate chips
¼ c. milk   club crackers

   Line a 9"x13" pan with a layer of club crackers. In a 3 quart pan, mix the sugars, butter, milk and crushed graham crackers. Spread this over the club crackers. Add another layer of club crackers. Melt peanut butter and chocolate chips together and spread over last layer of crackers. Cool and cut into squares.

Caramels*

Beachy's Bulk Foods

3 c. syrup   1¾ c. butter
4 c. heavy cream   ½ tsp. salt
4 c. sugar

   Cook together until 240° or 245° then add 2 teaspoons vanilla and pour in buttered cookie sheet. Cool and cut into pieces.

Chocolate Candies*

Beachy's Bulk Foods

Put water in bottom of double boiler. Heat water to boiling, remove from heat and put chocolate on top. May have to heat water several times, but always remove chocolate while heating water. When chocolate is melted, dip anything you like. Suggestions: peanuts, cashews, coconut, pretzels, or crackers with peanut butter.

Chocolate Scotcheroos

Melvin & Beth Ann Beachy

1 c. sugar	1 c. peanut butter
1 c. light corn syrup	6 c. Rice Krispies

Chocolate Topping:
6 oz. chocolate chips	6 oz. butterscotch chips

Cook sugar and corn syrup in 3 quart saucepan over medium heat until mixture boils. Immediately remove from heat. Stir in peanut butter. Mix in Rice Krispies. Press out on wax paper and spread chocolate topping over top and roll up. After it's cooled, slice and serve. *Chocolate Topping:* Melt over hot, but not boiling water. Blend well, then spread on top of Rice Krispie mixture.

Divinity Candy*

Beachy's Bulk Foods

2⅔ c. sugar   2 egg whites
⅔ c. Karo   1 tsp. vanilla
½ c. water

Cook sugar, Karo and water over low heat, stirring constantly until sugar is dissolved. Cook, without stirring, to hard ball stage. Beat egg whites until stiff and beat while pouring syrup in. Add vanilla. Beat until fluffy. Drop by spoonfuls onto wax paper. Do not make when there is high humidity.

Butterscotch Fudge

Levi & Katie Beachy

4 c. butterscotch chips   pinch of salt
1 can sweetened condensed milk   ½ tsp. maple flavoring
2 Tbsp. white vinegar   1 c. chopped walnuts

In a heavy saucepan, over low heat, melt butterscotch chips with milk. Remove from heat and stir in remaining ingredients. Spread evenly in an 8"x8" wax-paper lined pan. Chill 2–3 hours or until firm. Yield: 2½ lbs.

Chocolate Fudge

Levi & Katie Beachy

3 c. semisweet chocolate chips   1½ tsp. vanilla
1 can sweetened condensed milk   ½ c. chopped walnuts
dash of salt

In a heavy saucepan, over low heat, melt chocolate chips with milk. Remove from heat and stir in remaining ingredients. Spread evenly in wax-paper lined 8"x8" pan. Chill 2–3 hours or until firm. Turn fudge onto cutting board. Peel off paper and cut into squares. Store loosely covered at room temperature. Yield: 2 lbs.

Peanut Butter Fudge

Levi & Katie Beachy

2 c. peanut butter chips   dash of salt
1 can sweetened condensed milk   ½ c. chopped peanuts

In a heavy saucepan, melt chocolate chips. Remove from heat, and add rest of ingredients. Spread evenly into a wax-paper lined 8"x8" pan. Chill 2–3 hours or until firm. Yield: 1½ lbs.

White Confetti Fudge

Levi & Katie Beachy

1½ lb. white chocolate   1 tsp. vanilla
1 can sweetened condensed milk   1 c. chopped mixed candied fruit
pinch of salt

In a heavy saucepan, melt white chocolate with milk. Remove from heat and add rest of ingredients. Spread evenly into a wax-paper lined 8"x8" pan. Chill 2–3 hours or until firm. Yield: 2½ lbs.

Mock Twix Bars

Raymond & Martha Beachy

club crackers	¾ c. brown sugar
1 c. crushed graham crachers	⅓ c. milk
½ c. sugar	½ c. butter

Topping:

⅔ c. peanut butter	1 c. chocolate chips

Butter a 9"x13" pan. Place a layer of whole club crackers in pan. Boil next ingredients for 5 minutes. Place another layer of club crackers on top. *Topping:* Melt chocolate chips and peanut butter; spread over top.

Muddy Buddies

Edward Beachy

9 c. Corn or Rice Chex	¼ c. margarine
1 c. chocolate chips	1 tsp. vanilla
½ c. peanut butter	1½ c. powdered sugar

Pour cereal in bowl, set aside. In saucepan, over low heat melt chips, peanut butter and margarine until smooth, stirring often. Remove from heat, add vanilla. Pour over cereal. Stir until all pieces are coated evenly. Pour into a large plastic bag with powdered sugar. Shake until all pieces are well coated. Spread on wax paper to cool.

Maple Center Peanut Butter

Raymond & Martha Beachy

5 c. brown sugar, packed	1 Tbsp. glycerin
1 c. water	1½–2 tsp. maple flavoring
1 Tbsp. vinegar	5 lb. chocolate
½ c. Karo	4 lb. peanuts

Boil all ingredients except chocolate and peanuts together to 245°–250°. Pour in flat pan. Do not scrape out kettle. Let it set at room temperature until cool. Then stir in 2 well-beaten egg whites. Stir until creamy. It will get a dull look. Takes between ½–1½ hours to stir it to where you can form balls. Roll in balls, chill and dip in melted chocolate then cover with peanuts and chocolate.

Peanut Butter Balls

Gary Lynn Helmuth

½ lb. powdered sugar	24 oz. melting chocolate or
¼ c. butter	chocolate chips
½ c. peanut butter	peanut oil (optional)

Mix together powdered sugar, butter and peanut butter. Shape into balls. Melt chocolate in microwave, stirring often, add a few drops of peanut oil if needed to help thin the chocolate. Dip balls in chocolate and place on waxed paper to harden. Yield: 50 bite-size balls.

Party Mints
Levi & Katie Beachy

8 oz. cream cheese   food coloring
1 tsp. flavoring   6⅔ c. powdered sugar

Have cream cheese at room temperature and mash up with wooden spoon. Add flavoring and coloring. Mix evenly. Add powdered sugar a little at a time, finally kneading into a ball with your hands. Pinch off pieces and roll into marble-sized balls. Roll in granulated sugar, then press into mold. Unmold at once on waxed paper, just tap the back of the mold to make the mint come out.

Peppermint Patties
Joseph & Melissa Beachy

8 oz. cream cheese   peppermint flavoring
½ tsp. vanilla   powdered sugar, enough to be
dash of salt   able to roll in balls

Mix cream cheese and flavorings; add salt. Mix well, then add powdered sugar. Make into patties, chill, then coat with chocolate.

Swallow your pride occasionally—its not fattening.

Party Mix

Robert & Dorothy Beachy
Mary Lorene Beachy

12 oz. Honey Comb
12 oz. Cheerios
¾–1 bag pretzel sticks
1 box Bugles

1 box Chicken in a Biskit crackers
Cheetos
4 oz. shoestring potatoes
Fruit Loops (optional)

Sauce:
1 pkg. spaghetti sauce mix
1 pkg. Ranch dressing mix
2 Tbsp. Worcestershire sauce

1 c. butter
¾ c. vegetable oil

Mix together sauce ingredients; and mix to cereal mixture except for Chicken in a Biskit crackers and Cheetos. (Add the last 20 minutes of baking time.) Bake in oven at 200° for 2 hours, stirring every 15 minutes. Yield: 13 quarts.

Party Mix

Levi & Katie Beachy

¼ c. margarine
1¼ tsp. seasoned salt
4½ tsp. Worcestershire sauce
4 c. Corn Chex

4 c. Rice Chex
1 c. salted mixed nuts
1 c. pretzel sticks

Preheat oven to 250°. In a saucepan, melt margarine, salt and Worcestershire sauce. Mix together rest of ingredients in a large bowl or roasting pan. Pour margarine mixture over cereal mixture. Mix well. Bake 1 hour, stirring every 15 minutes. Cool, then store in airtight container.

Party Mix

Melvin & Beth Ann Beachy

4 c. Rice Chex, rounded
4 c. Corn Chex, rounded
1 box pretzels
6 c. Cheerios
6 c. Kix
1 lb. salted peanuts

1 c. butter
2 Tbsp. Worcestershire sauce
2 tsp. Lawry's seasoning salt
2 tsp. celery salt
1 tsp. salt

Mix together first 6 ingredients. Melt rest of ingredients together and add to cereal mixture. Bake at 250° for 1 hour. Stir every 15 minutes.

Honey Mustard Pretzels

Mary Lorene Beachy

2 lb. pretzels
¾ c. vegetable oil
4 Tbsp. honey mustard powder

3 Tbsp. sour cream and
    onion powder
2 Tbsp. Ranch dressing mix

Heat oil (not to boiling); add powders. Stir briskly until well mixed. Pour over pretzels in a large bowl and mix well. Bake at 260° for 30 minutes, stirring every 15 minutes.

Deluxe Party Mix

Brandon Beachy

10 c. Cheerios
16 c. Crispix
5 c. Bugles
5 c. pretzel sticks
5 c. Golden Graham cereal

5 c. mixed nuts
12 oz. Orville Reidenbachers
    popcorn oil
1 pkg. Hidden Valley Ranch
    dressing mix

Mix together first 6 ingredients in a large bowl. Mix together oil and dressing mix and stir over low heat until warm. Pour oil mixture over dry mix and toss until evenly coated. Add a bag of cheese curls. Yield: 3 gallons.

Peanut Butter Party Mix

Joseph & Melissa Beachy

2 Tbsp. butter
⅓ c. creamy peanut butter
2 c. Wheat Chex cereal

2 c. Rice Chex cereal
¼ c. dry roasted peanuts

Melt butter; add peanut butter, stir until mixed well. Toss cereals and nuts in peanut butter mixture until coated. Remove from heat. Spread on ungreased cookie sheet. Bake at 375° for 8 minutes or until golden brown. Drain on paper towels.

Caramel Corn Pops

Orvan & Marilyn Miller

8 oz. bag corn pops

Caramel Sauce:

1 c. butter (not margarine)	½ c. light corn syrup
1 c. brown sugar	1 tsp. soda

Pour corn pops in a large roaster pan. *Caramel Sauce:* In a 2 quart saucepan cook butter, brown sugar and corn syrup together for 2 minutes; add soda to mixture. This will cause to foam, so a 2 quart saucepan is necessary. Pour caramel mixture over corn pops and stir until mixed. Bake at 250° for 45 minutes. Stir at least every 10–15 minutes. Remove from oven and pour on wax paper. Break apart as soon as removing from oven.

Caramel Popcorn

Levi & Katie Beachy

2 gal. popcorn	½ c. light corn syrup
½ c. butter	1 tsp. salt
½ c. margarine	1 tsp. maple flavoring
1¾ c. brown sugar	½ tsp. soda

Mix butter, margarine, sugar, corn syrup and salt together and bring to a boil. Boil for 5 minutes. Then add maple flavoring and soda. Stir until foamy. Pour over popcorn; stir well. Bake at 250° for 1 hour, stirring every 15 minutes.

Crunchy Peanut Popcorn

Raymond & Martha Beachy

1½ gal. popcorn
¼ c. margarine
16 marshmallows

¾ c. brown sugar, packed
dash of salt
¼ c. crunchy peanut butter

Combine margarine, marshmallows, brown sugar and salt in saucepan; cook over low heat until dissolved. Add peanut butter, and stir. Pour over popcorn. Stir until evenly coated.

Crispy Cinnamon Popcorn

Melvin & Beth Ann Beachy

7 qt. popcorn

Sauce:

1 c. sugar
½ c. Karo
1 c. margarine
1 tsp. salt

1 c. cinnamon imperials
1 tsp. vanilla
½ tsp. soda

In a heavy saucepan, melt sugar, Karo, margarine, salt and cinnamon imperials; stir until dissolved. Boil 5 minutes then turn off heat and add vanilla and soda. Stir well. Pour over popcorn and mix well. Place on cookie sheets and bake at 250° for 1 hour, stirring every 10–15 minutes. When cold, store in airtight container.

Jell-O Popcorn Balls

Marnita Beachy

¼ c. melted butter   1 sm. pkg. Jell-O
½ lb. marshmallows   6½ qt. popped popcorn

Melt marshmallows in melted butter; add Jell-O and mix with popcorn. Shape into balls.

Jolly Jell-O Popcorn Balls

Gary Lynn Helmuth

¾ c. sugar   1½ oz. Jell-O, any flavor
¾ c. Karo

Pop corn and sort out any unpopped corn. Mix sugar, syrup and Jell-O; bring to a full boil. Cool, slightly and pour over popped corn. Stir well. Butter hands and quickly mold into balls. Will get hard very fast. Cool and enjoy.

Peanut Butter Popcorn

Matthew David Miller

½ c. popcorn (unpopped)   3 Tbsp. margarine
3 Tbsp. peanut butter   3 Tbsp. brown sugar

Pop popcorn. Melt together peanut butter, margarine and brown sugar. Do not boil. Pour peanut butter mixture over popcorn, stir well. Bake at 250° for 1 hour, stirring every 15 minutes.

Rice Krispie Candy

Merlyn Jay Helmuth

½ c. butter

1 pkg. or 4 c. miniature
  marshmallows

5 c. Rice Krispie cereal

Melt butter in large saucepan over low heat. Add marshmallows and stir until melted and well blended. Cook slowly 2 minutes longer, stirring constantly. Remove from heat and add cereal until well coated. Press in buttered pan. Cut when cool.

Rock Candy*

Beachy's Bulk Foods

2½ c. syrup

2½ c. water

7 c. sugar

2 tsp. cinnamon or whatever
  flavor you want

add coloring

Mix together syrup, water and sugar; then cook to 300°. Remove from heat and add flavoring and coloring. Pour on buttered cookie sheets and lay in powdered sugar when cool enough to handle and cut into small pieces with scissors.

Desserts

Apple Crisp

Orvan & Marilyn Miller

½ c. sugar
2 Tbsp. flour
¼ tsp. salt

1 tsp. cinnamon
1½ qt. apples, sliced

Top Part:
1 c. oatmeal
1 c. brown sugar
1 c. flour

¼ tsp. soda
½ tsp. baking powder
⅔ c. butter

Mix sugar, flour, salt and cinnamon. Add to apples and mix. Put on bottom of a greased pan. Mix the ingredients of top part until crumbly, then put on apples and pat firmly. Bake at 350° until brown and crust is formed. Serve with milk or cream. It is delicious hot or cold.

Apple Dumplings

Alvin & Charlene Kanagy

2 tubes crescent rolls
2 baking apples,
   cut into 8 slices each
¾ c. margarine

1½ c. sugar
1 tsp. cinnamon
12 oz. Mountain Dew

Separate rolls into 16 pieces. Place 1 apple slice in each. Roll up from large end to small. Place side by side in a 9"x13" pan. Melt margarine and mix with sugar and cinnamon. Spoon over dumplings then pour Mountain Dew over all. Bake at 350° for 45 minutes.

Apple Dumplings

Treva Kay Beachy

6 apples, peeled and cut in half

Dough:

2 c. flour

2½ tsp. baking powder

½ tsp. salt

⅔ c. shortening

½ c. milk

Sauce:

2 c. brown sugar

2 c. water

¼ c. butter

½ tsp. cinnamon

Roll out dough; cut in squares. Place one apple half on each square. Wet edges of dough and press into a ball around the apple. Set dumplings in a pan. Pour sauce over dumplings and bake. Bake at 350° for 35–40 minutes or until golden brown and apples are soft when pricked with a fork.

Apple Fritters

Willard & Carol Ann Helmuth

1 beaten egg

1 c. milk

1 c. finely chopped apples

¼ c. sugar

¼ tsp. salt

½ tsp. vanilla

1 Tbsp. baking powder

2 c. flour

vegetable oil (for frying)

powdered sugar

In a mixing bowl, combine beaten egg, milk, chopped apples, sugar, salt and vanilla. Stir together flour and baking powder; fold into egg mixture, stirring just until all flour is moistened. Drop batter by rounded teaspoonfuls into hot oil (350°). Fry until deep golden brown, about 3–4 minutes turning once. Drain fritters thoroughly on paper towels. Roll in powdered sugar or sift sugar over tops.

Banana Split Brownie Pizza

Marnita Beachy

1 pkg. brownie mix
16 oz. cream cheese,
  softened
⅔ c. sugar
8 oz. crushed pineapples,
  drained

2–3 bananas
strawberries
½ c. chopped nuts
1 oz. semisweet chocolate
1 Tbsp. margarine

Preheat oven to 375°. Prepare brownie mix according to directions on box. Put on pizza pan. Bake 15–20 minutes or until set. Cool. Mix cream cheese and sugar until smooth. Spread over brownie crust. Place the crushed pineapples on cream cheese layer. Slice bananas (put in lemon juice) and strawberries and place on cream cheese layer. Sprinkle with chopped nuts. Melt chocolate and butter together; drizzle over pizza.

Note: Can also make brownies from scratch.

Seven prayerless days makes one weak.

Fruit Pizza

Willard & Carol Ann Helmuth

Crust:

¾ c. margarine

1 c. sugar

2 eggs, beaten

1½ tsp. baking powder

⅜ tsp. salt

¾ tsp. vanilla

Cream Cheese Mixture:

8 oz. cream cheese

¾ c. powdered sugar

2 c. whipped topping

Sauce:

½ c. orange juice

¾ c. sugar

1½ c. water

2 Tbsp. perma-flo

1 Tbsp. lemon juice

Crust: Blend margarine and sugar; add eggs. Stir in baking powder, salt, vanilla and flour. Spread on cookie sheet and bake at 375° for 12 minutes. Cool crust and top with cream cheese mixture. *Cream Cheese Mixture:* Mix cream cheese and powdered sugar until fluffy then add topping. Top with your favorite fruit then put fruit sauce on top. *Sauce:* Mix everything together cold; then heat until boiling, stirring constantly. Cool; pour over fruit.

A pinch of salt added to cream before whipping strengthens the fat cells and makes them more elastic. This helps the cream stiffen much more quickly.

Fruit Pizza

Anna Viola Beachy

Crust:

1 c. flour   ½ c. butter, melted
½ c. chopped nuts

Filling:

8 oz. cream cheese, softened   1 c. powdered sugar
2 c. Cool Whip

Sauce:

½ c. orange juice   ¼ c. water
½ c. sugar   1 Tbsp. perma-flo
1 Tbsp. lemon juice

Crust: Mix well, and press into a 9"x13" pan. Bake at 375° for 15 minutes. Cool. *Filling:* Mix cream cheese and powdered sugar, fold in whipped topping. Spread on cooled crust, let set until firm. Arrange fruit on top, frozen mixed fruit, or drained fruit cocktail, or fresh fruit tastes the best. *Sauce:* Mix together juice, sugar and lemon juice, bring to a boil. Mix together water and perma-flo. Gradually pour into juice. Cook sauce, cool, then pour over fruit. Refrigerate 4 hours. Serve.

Fruit Pizza Crust

Steve & Lorene Helmuth

1½ c. powdered sugar   ½ tsp. salt
1 c. butter   2½ c. Gold Medal flour
1 egg   1 tsp. cream of tartar
1 tsp. almond flavoring

Mix together and bake at 350°. Do not overbake. Enough for 1 cookie sheet.

Rhubarb Pizza

Renita Faye Helmuth

Layer 1:

1 c. flour	2 Tbsp. butter
1 tsp. baking powder	1 egg
¼ tsp. cream of tartar	2 Tbsp. milk
¼ c. sugar	

Layer 2:

3 c. fresh cut-up rhubarb	3 oz. strawberry Jell-O

Layer 3:

1 c. sugar	⅓ c. butter
½ c. flour	

Combine ingredients of first layer, mix, knead and press into greased 9"x13" pan. Then top with cut-up rhubarb and sprinkle dry Jell-O over top. Combine third layer ingredients for crumb topping. Bake at 350° for 40–45 minutes.

Strawberry Pizza

Abner & Sovilla Mae Zook

1 c. margarine	½ tsp. baking powder
1½ c. flour	½ c. powdered sugar

Filling:

8 oz. cream cheese	9 oz. Cool Whip
1 c. powdered sugar	

Spray cookie sheet and spread crust in with spatula. Bake at 350° for 15 minutes or until light brown. *Filling:* Soften cream cheese and mix in powdered sugar and fold in Cool Whip. Spread on cooled crust. Spread 1 quart strawberry filling on top.

Taffy Apple Pizza

Alvin & Charlene Kanagy

1 pkg. refrigerated sugar
    cookie dough, softened
8 oz. cream cheese, softened
¼ c. brown sugar
¼ c. creamy peanut butter
½ tsp. vanilla

2 or 3 Granny Smith apples
lemon juice
cinnamon
¼ c. caramel ice cream topping
½ c. chopped peanuts

Press dough on a 15" round pizza pan about ¼" thick. Bake 16–18 minutes. Cool completely. Combine cream cheese, brown sugar, peanut butter and vanilla; mix well. Spread on top of cookie dough. Peel, core and slice apples. Sprinkle with lemon juice, then arrange over cream cheese mixture. Sprinkle with cinnamon. Drizzle caramel topping over apples then top with peanuts.

Triple Berry Brownie Pizza

Joseph & Melissa Beachy

1 pkg. fudge brownie mix
1 tsp. almond extract
8 oz. cream cheese
1 Tbsp. sugar
1 tsp. vanilla

½ tsp. grated lemon peel
2 c. whipped topping
mixed fresh berries, blackberries,
    blueberries, strawberries

Prepare brownie batter according to directions on box; adding almond extract. Spread into a greased 14" pizza pan. Bake at 375° for 15–18 minutes. Cool on wire rack. In a large mixing bowl, beat cream cheese, sugar, vanilla and lemon peel until smooth. Fold in whipped topping. Spread over crust to within ½" of edges. Top with berries. Refrigerate for 2–3 hours before serving.

Angel Food Ice Box Cake

Levi & Katie Beachy

1 pkg. raspberry or strawberry Jell-O	2 c. cream
1 c. hot water	1 c. crushed pineapples
½ c. sugar	12 lg. marshmallows
	1 angel food cake

Mix Jell-O and sugar; add hot water. Cool until it starts to thicken. Beat well, add cream which you have beaten stiff. To beaten Jell-O, add pineapples and marshmallows, cut fine. Slice cake in thin slices into a large pan. Arrange 3 alternate layers.

Blueberry Buckle

Joseph & Melissa Beachy

¾ c. sugar	2 c. flour
¼ c. margarine, softened	2 tsp. baking powder
1 egg	¼ tsp. salt
½ c. milk	2 c. blueberries, well drained

Crumbs:

½ c. sugar	½ tsp. cinnamon
½ c. flour	¼ c. butter, softened

Thoroughly mix sugar, margarine and egg. Stir in milk. Sift together dry ingredients and mix with the rest of the ingredients. Carefully blend in the blueberries. Spread into a greased 9"x9" pan. *Crumbs:* Mix sugar, flour and cinnamon; cut in butter until crumbly. Sprinkle on top of batter. Bake at 375° for 25–30 minutes. Serve warm with milk.

Butterscotch Pudding

Orvan & Marilyn Miller

1½ c. brown sugar   5 Tbsp. flour, rounded
¼ c. butter   4 c. milk
6 Tbsp. cream   salt
2 eggs   vanilla

Crumbs:
2 c. flour   ¾ c. butter
½ c. brown sugar   pinch of salt
nuts, if desired   pinch of soda
½ c. sugar

Boil together brown sugar, butter and cream for 5 minutes. Mix together eggs, flour and milk; stir into first mixture and boil a few minutes; add a pinch of salt and vanilla. *Crumbs:* Mix together and bake until light brown. Chop up before its cold. Put on layers; pudding, crumbs and whipped topping.

Banana Slush

Melvin & Beth Ann Beachy

2 c. sugar   1 can crushed pineapples
3 c. water   8 bananas
6 oz. orange juice (mix like can)

Boil sugar and water for 5 minutes. Remove from heat and cool completely. Then add rest of ingredients. Freeze. When ready to serve, let thaw until slushy.

Cherry Berry on a Cloud

Orvan & Marilyn Miller

3 egg whites
¼ tsp. cream of tartar

¾ c. sugar

Filling:
8 oz. cream cheese
1 c. Cool Whip or
   whipped cream

1 c. powdered sugar
cherry pie filling

Heat oven to 275°. Cover cookie sheet with brown paper bag. Beat egg whites and cream of tartar until stiff. Add sugar, beat a little more. Shape into a circle on pan and kind of hollow out in middle. Leave a ridge around the edge. Bake 1½ hours. Turn off oven, leave in at least 1 more hour. If you want it to fit nicely on a cake platter, bake on pizza pan. You can also use other kinds of pie filling.

Frozen Chocolate Mint Squares

Wilmer & Sarah Beachy

1½ c. finely crushed chocolate
   wafers
6 Tbsp. butter
7 oz. marshmallow creme
½ tsp. mint extract

green food coloring
2 c. whipping cream
¾ c. miniature semisweet
   chocolate chips, divided

Combine crushed wafers and butter and press into 9"x9" pan. Beat marshmallows creme, extract and green food coloring until smooth. Fold in ½ cup chocolate chips. Whip cream until soft peaks form, fold into marshmallow creme mixture. Spread over crust. Sprinkle remaining chips on top. Freeze at least 6 hours.

Chocolate Peanut Butter Dessert

Steve & Lorene Helmuth

Crust:

2 c. flour	¼ c. sugar
1 c. margarine	1 tsp. salt

Crumbs:

2 c. powdered sugar	⅔ c. peanut butter

Pudding:

6 c. milk, divided	5 Tbsp. cornstarch
1½ c. sugar	2 Tbsp. flour
¼ c. cocoa	4 eggs
1 tsp. salt	

Crust: Blend ingredients until crumbly. Press into a 9"x13" cake pan and bake at 325° for 30–35 minutes. Cool. *Crumbs:* Mix ingredients together to form balls. *Pudding:* Heat 4 cups milk. Mix sugar, cocoa, salt, cornstarch and flour; add beaten eggs and 2 cups cold milk. Add to boiling milk and cook. Cool. Line baked and cooled crust with crumbs. Add pudding. Top with whipped cream and sprinkle with more crumbs. Delicious!

Deliciously Rich Chocolate Pudding

Joseph & Melissa Beachy

2 c. chocolate chips	1 c. milk
⅓ c. sugar	¼ c. butter

Put chocolate chips and sugar in blender and chop until chips are coarsely chopped. Over medium heat, bring milk and butter to a boil, add to blender and mix until smooth. Refrigerate. Garnish with a dab of whipped topping before serving.

Lemon Delight

Orvan & Marilyn Miller

First Layer:
1 c. flour
½ c. butter or margarine
¾ c. nuts, chopped

Second Layer:
8 oz. cream cheese
1 c. powdered sugar
1 c. Cool Whip or whipped topping

Third Layer:
2 sm. pkg. (or ⅔ c.) lemon instant pudding
3 c. milk

First Layer: Press into a 9"x13" pan, bake at 350° for 20 minutes. Cool completely before adding next layer. *Second Layer:* Mix well and put on top of cooled crust. *Third Layer:* Beat until thick. Spread on top of second layer. Top with Cool Whip and nuts if desired. Cool and serve.

Note: Butterscotch instant pudding is also delicious!

Hasty Pudding

Wesley & Martha Beachy

Dough:
⅓ c. brown sugar
2 Tbsp. butter
1 c. flour
1½ tsp. baking powder
¼ tsp. salt
½ c. milk
1 c. raisins

Syrup:
1 c. brown sugar
½ Tbsp. flour
2 c. water
1 tsp. vanilla

Mix dough ingredients together and place in pan. Bring syrup to a boil and pour over dough.

Grape Nut Pudding

Abner & Sovilla Mae Zook

4 c. milk, divided
½ c. brown sugar
3 Tbsp. flour
2 eggs

1 c. Grape Nuts
1 c. raisins
maple flavoring
whipped topping

Bring 3 cups milk and brown sugar to a boil. Mix 1 cup milk, flour and egg yolks and stir in hot milk mixture. Boil. Add Grape Nuts, maple flavoring and raisins. Beat egg whites and stir into pudding. After pudding is cooled, add topping.

Toffee Coffee Blizzards

Alvin & Charlene Kanagy

1¼ c. milk, divided
¼ c. sugar
1 Tbsp. cornstarch, rounded
1 Tbsp. instant coffee
1 tsp. vanilla
1 Tbsp. butter

1 can sweetened condensed milk
2 c. Rich's topping
12 oz. English Heath toffee bits
12 Oreo cookies
caramel and chocolate ice cream
  syrup

In a saucepan, heat 1 cup milk to boiling point. In the meantime; combine sugar, cornstarch and coffee. Mix in ¼ cup milk and slowly add to hot milk, stirring constantly. Bring to a boil and boil 1 minute or until thickened. Remove from heat and add vanilla and butter. Cool completely; add sweetened condensed milk and whip topping. Fold into pudding. Add Heath bits and crushed cookies into a 9"x13" pan. Pour pudding mixtures over cookies. Swirl with caramel and chocolate syrup. Freeze overnight or longer.

Note: A great make ahead dessert. I crush 20 cookies and use a 9"x13" pan.

Oreo Pudding

Levi & Katie Beachy

1 pkg. Oreo cookies
12 oz. Cool Whip

½ gal. vanilla ice cream, softened

Crush the cookies, put some in bottom of a 9"x13" pan. Mix the rest of crumbs with other ingredients, then pour mixture on top of crumbs in pan and freeze.

Frozen Peanut Butter Pudding

Steve & Lorene Helmuth

4 oz. cream cheese
1 c. powdered sugar
½ c. peanut butter

½ c. milk
8 oz. whipped cream
9" graham cracker crust

Beat cream cheese until soft and fluffy. Beat in sugar and peanut butter. Slowly add milk, blending thoroughly into mixture. Fold in whipped cream. Pour into graham cracker crust. Freeze until firm.

Hint: Have you had your instant puddings tasting sour? To prevent this, use store boughten milk or if using raw milk heat milk until scalding, then cool until cold. Then mix with instant puddings.

Creamy Raspberry Delight

Renita Faye Helmuth

1 c. graham cracker crumbs
¼ c. butter, melted

3 Tbsp. sugar

Filling:
10 oz. frozen raspberries or
  any berries
⅓ c. cold water
8 oz. cream cheese

1 Tbsp. unflavored gelatin
½ c. sugar
1 c. whip topping, whipped

Combine crumbs, sugar and butter; press into a 8 or 9" pan. Bake at 350° for 10 minutes. Cool. Meanwhile for filling; drain berries and reserve juice, set berries aside. In a saucepan, combine juice, cold water and gelatin. Let set 5 minutes. Cook and stir over low heat until gelatin dissolves. Remove from heat. Cool. Beat cream cheese and sugar; add berries and gelatin mixture. Beat on low until blended, chill until partially set. Watch carefully as mixture will set quickly, gently fold in whip cream, spoon into crust. Top with fresh berries and whip cream.

Pink Velvet

Renita Faye Helmuth

1½ c. graham crackers
¼ c. brown sugar
2 Tbsp. melted margarine
1 pkg. Jell-O

1 c. hot water
¼ c. sugar
1 c. whipped topping

Mix together first 3 ingredients. Reserve ⅓ cup crumb mixture. Dissolve Jell-O in hot water. Add sugar and chill until partially set; whip Jell-O until fluffy. Fold in 1 cup whipped topping. Pour over crust. Sprinkle reserved crumbs on top. Chill until set.

Rhubarb Delight

Renita Faye Helmuth

Crust:

2 c. flour   1 c. margarine
2 Tbsp. sugar

Filling:

6 c. rhubarb   1 c. whip cream
2¼ c. sugar   4 egg whites
¾ c. water   ¼ tsp. salt
⅔ c. Jell-O   2 tsp. vanilla

Crust: Mix all ingredients and press into pan. Bake crust 15–20 minutes. *Filling:* Simmer rhubarb, sugar and water until rhubarb is tender. Add Jell-O and stir until dissolved. Let cool until about set. Add whip cream and stiffly beaten egg whites, salt and vanilla. Pour on baked crust. Let set for 2 hours.

Frozen Pumpkin Dessert

Wilmer & Sarah Beachy

Crust:

1½ c. crushed ginger snaps   ¼ c. melted butter
1 Tbsp. sugar

Filling:

2 c. ice cream   ½ tsp. ginger
1 c. pumpkin   ½ tsp. cinnamon
1 c. powdered sugar   ¼ tsp. nutmeg
½ tsp. salt   1 c. whipped cream

Mix crust ingredients and press into a 9" pan. Bake at 300° for 15 minutes. Cool. Place ice cream on crust. Mix together remaining ingredients and pour over ice cream. Freeze for at least 2 hours. Top with additional whipped topping.

Pumpkin Pie Dessert Squares

LaWayne Ray Helmuth

Crust:

1 c. flour	½ c. sugar
¼ tsp. salt	½ c. butter
1¼ tsp. baking powder	1 egg

Filling:

4 c. pumpkin	4 eggs
5 tsp. pumpkin pie spice	1⅓ c. milk
1 c. brown sugar	

Topping:

1 c. reserved crumbs	¼ c. sugar
1 tsp. cinnamon	¼ c. margarine

Crust: Mix flour, salt, baking powder and sugar; reserve 1 cup crumbs. Combine melted butter and egg with rest of crumbs. Press into a 9"x13" pan. Mix filling ingredients in order given. Pour over crust. Make topping and sprinkle over filling. Bake at 350° for 50 minutes.

Pumpkin Yummy

Joseph & Melissa Beachy

1 qt. pumpkin	3 eggs
1 c. brown sugar	1 can evaporated milk
2 tsp. cinnamon	1½ c. milk
½ tsp. ginger	1 yellow cake mix
¼ tsp. nutmeg	¾ c. butter, melted

Combine first 5 ingredients; beat in eggs and milk until smooth. Pour into a 9"x13" pan. Sprinkle dry cake mix over the mixture, drizzle melted butter over cake mix. Bake at 350° for 50 minutes. Cool and serve with whipped topping.

Velvety Custard

Raymond & Martha Beachy

4 eggs, slightly beaten
½ c. sugar
1 tsp. vanilla

¼ tsp. salt
2½ c. milk, scalded

Thoroughly mix eggs, sugar, vanilla and salt. Slowly stir in the scalded milk. Make 2–2½ batches for a 9"x13" glass pan. Set your pan of custard into a larger pan of water to bake. Bake at 350° until set. Be careful not to let the custard cook. You may also use this for pie.

Custard

Wesley & Martha Beachy

5½ c. milk
1 Tbsp. unflavored gelatin
7 lg. eggs, divided

¼ c. sugar
1½ c. brown sugar
½ tsp. salt

Soften gelatin in ½ cup milk and heat remaining 5 cups. Add gelatin and stir until dissolved. Beat 3 egg whites with ¼ cup sugar until stiff. Set aside. Combine salt and rest of eggs, brown sugar and salt. Slowly add hot milk mixture and mix well. Fold in beaten egg white mixture. Pour this into a pan. Set it into another pan with hot water. Bake at 325° for 40 minutes or until knife comes out clean.

Cheesecake

Anna Viola Beachy

Step 1:

1 pkg. (⅓ c.) Jell-O   1 c. boiling water

Step 2:

30 graham crackers, crushed   1 Tbsp. brown sugar
½ c. margarine, softened

Step 3:

8 oz. cream cheese, softened   1 c. sugar
1 tsp. vanilla

Step 4:

1 can Milnot, chilled

Step 1: Mix Jell-O and boiling water, cool. You can use lemon, raspberry or strawberry flavor. *Step 2:* Crush graham crackers very fine, add margarine and brown sugar and mix. Line a 9"x13" pan with the crumbs. *Step 3:* Mix cream cheese and vanilla. Mix well and add sugar. Add this mixture to Jell-O. Mix well. *Step 4:* Whip Milnot until soft peaks form. Fold in Jell-O and cream cheese mixture until it's well blended. Pour over graham cracker crust and add a few crushed crackers on top. Chill 12 hours.

It's-A-Snap Cheesecake
Marnita Beachy

1 env. unflavored gelatin
½ c. sugar
1 c. boiling water
16 oz. cream cheese, softened

1 tsp. vanilla
1 tsp. pineapple flavoring
blueberries (optional)

Mix gelatin and sugar in a small bowl; add boiling water and stir until dissolved. Beat cream cheese and flavorings in a large bowl with mixer until smooth. Slowly beat in gelatin mixture. Pour in pan and top with berries. Refrigerate until firm.

Creamy Mocha Frozen Dessert
Treva Kay Beachy

1 Tbsp. hot water
2 tsp. instant coffee
1 c. Oreo cookie crumbs
8 oz. cream cheese
½ c. sugar

1 can sweetened condensed milk
¼ c. Nesquik chocolate
8 oz. Cool Whip
½ gal. ice cream, softened

Dissolve coffee granules in hot water, set aside. Pat crushed cookies in a 9"x13" pan. Beat cream cheese and sugar; then add rest of ingredients. Freeze for about 2 hours, then get out and garnish with Oreo crumbs and chocolate syrup. Then freeze hard.

Mocha Cheesecake

Alvin & Charlene Kanagy

2¼ c. Oreo cookies
½ c. butter, melted
8 oz. cream cheese
1 can sweetened condensed milk

½ c. chocolate syrup
8 oz. Cool Whip
2 tsp. instant coffee
1 Tbsp. hot water

Crush Oreo cookies; mix with melted butter and put in bottom of a 9"x13" pan. Reserve some for top. Mix together cream cheese, sweetened condensed milk and chocolate syrup. Then add Cool Whip; mix well. Mix instant coffee with hot water; mix into pudding, spread on top of cookies and put rest of cookies on top. Good chilled or frozen. I make a double batch for a 9"x13" pan.

Caramel Ice Cream Dessert

Abner & Sovilla Mae Zook

1 c. brown sugar
1½ c. butter
1¼ c. quick oats
3 c. flour

¾ c. pecans
1 gal. vanilla ice cream
caramel or butterscotch
    ice cream topping

Mix sugar, butter, oats, flour and pecans. Bake at 350° until golden brown; stir. Put ½ of crumbs in a 9"x13" pan. Put ice cream over crumbs. Drizzle ice cream topping over ice cream and put remaining crumbs on top. Freeze.

Oreo Pudding

Rosina Helmuth

Crumbs:

1 lg. pkg. Oreo cookies, crushed   ½ c. butter, melted

Pudding:

8 oz. cream cheese   12 oz. Cool Whip

3 c. milk   1 c. powdered sugar

2 pkg. instant vanilla pudding

Line bottom of 9"x13" pan with crumbs. Reserve some for top. Mix cream cheese and powdered sugar. Mix instant pudding and milk. Add to cream cheese. Add Cool Whip and pour on top of crumbs. Top with more Cool Whip and crumbs.

Baby Pearl Tapioca

6 c. water   1 c. sugar

pinch of salt   1 c. whipped cream

1 c. baby pearl tapioca   fruit

⅓ c. Jell-O

Bring water and salt to a boil; add tapioca. Bring to a boil again. Put lid on and turn off heat. Let set 1 hour or longer. Add any flavor Jell-O and sugar. Cool. Add whipped cream and fruit of any kind. Serves 12–15.

Chocolate Tapioca Pudding

Renita Faye Helmuth

¼ c. cocoa
4 c. boiling water
1 c. baby pearl tapioca
1 c. sugar
pinch of salt

½ c. cold water
1 tsp. vanilla
2–4 c. whipped topping
chopped nuts
candy bars

Mix cocoa and a little bit of hot water in a heavy saucepan; mix until smooth. Add rest of hot water and bring to a boil. Add tapioca and boil until almost clear. Add the sugar, salt, cold water and cool. When cold add vanilla, whip topping, nuts and cut-up candy bars. Mix well.

Large Pearl Tapioca

6 c. water
pinch of salt
1½ c. pearl tapioca
1 c. sugar

1 tsp. vanilla or ⅓ c. Jell-O
1 c. whipped cream
bananas or fruit of any kind

Bring water and salt to a boil; add tapioca. Bring to a boil and boil 45 minutes on low heat with lid on. Stir occasionally. Turn off heat and let set 1 hour. Drain off liquid and add sugar and vanilla or Jell-O. When ready to serve; add whipped cream and bananas, or fruit of any kind. Serves 12.

Fluffy Tapioca Pudding

Wilmer & Sarah Beachy

2 c. milk
3 Tbsp. minute tapioca
3 Tbsp. sugar
dash of salt
1 egg, separated

½ c. milk
2 Tbsp. sugar
¾ tsp. vanilla
¼ tsp. maple flavoring

Heat 2 cups milk to boiling. Mix together tapioca, 3 tablespoons sugar, salt, beaten egg yolk and ½ cup milk. Add to boiling milk, cook until thickened. Add beaten egg whites and 2 tablespoons sugar, stirring quickly until blended. Stir in flavorings. Let cool, then add whipped topping to your liking.

Note: To keep from burning, sprinkle 2 tablespoons sugar on top of milk before heating. DO NOT STIR.

Rhubarb Tapioca

Melvin & Beth Ann Beachy

3 qt. water
1 qt. rhubarb
2¼ c. sugar

1 tsp. salt
⅔ c. Jell-O
1 c. tapioca

Bring water to a boil. Add rhubarb and if using pearl tapioca, also add tapioca. Boil on medium-low for 15 minutes, stirring occasionally. Then add sugar, salt and Jell-O. (If using minute tapioca, add with sugar and boil a few minutes.) Remove from heat and chill, or ladle in jars and hot water bath for 10 minutes. Is good to eat with cake or cookies.

Pearl Tapioca

2 qt. milk
¾ c. sugar
½ c. tapioca, heaping

3 eggs, beaten
¾ c. sugar
¾ tsp. vanilla

Soak tapioca overnight; drain. Mix milk and sugar. Bring to a boil. Add tapioca. Cook and stir until tapioca is clear (at least 30 minutes). Then combine eggs, sugar and vanilla. Add to first mixture and bring to a full boil. Yield: 2 quarts.

Tapioca Small Pearl

½ c. tapioca
½ c. milk
1½ c. milk

3 egg yolks
⅓ c. sugar
⅛ tsp. salt

Soak tapioca in ½ c. milk, refrigerate for 10 minutes (or until milk is absorbed). Add the soaked tapioca and 1½ c. milk to rest of ingredients and stir together. Cook mixture in top of double boiler for 15–20 minutes. Allow tapioca to cool. Beat egg whites until stiff, but not dry. Gently fold egg whites into cooled tapioca. Chill and serve. *Variations:* Add ½ cup raisins, or 1 teaspoon grated orange rind, or ¼ cup coconut.

Seed Pearl Tapioca

½ c. tapioca
1 qt. milk
¾ c. sugar

3 eggs, beaten
¾ c. sugar
¾ tsp. vanilla

Soak tapioca overnight. Mix milk and sugar. Bring to a boil. Add tapioca, cook and stir until tapioca is clear, at least 30 minutes. Then combine eggs, sugar and vanilla. Add to above mixture and bring to a full boil. Yield: 2 quarts.

Small Pearl Tapioca

Wesley & Martha Beachy
Robert & Dorothy Beachy

2 qt. boiling water
1 tsp. salt
1½ c. sugar

1¼ c. sm. pearl tapioca
⅔ c. raspberry Jell-O

Bring water to boiling. Add sugar and salt. Bring to boil again. Add tapioca. Simmer for 20 minutes, stirring occasionally. Add Jell-O; stir until dissolved, then let set without stirring for 20 minutes. Cool; stirring occasionally. Before serving stir in 2 cups Cool Whip or more, depending how creamy you want it.

Easy Crockpot Tapioca

Wilmer & Sarah Beachy

8 c. milk
1½ c. sugar
1 c. pearl tapioca

4 eggs, beaten
2 tsp. vanilla
¼ tsp. maple flavoring

Put milk, sugar and tapioca in crockpot and stir. Cook on high for 3 hours, stirring occasionally. Add a little hot milk from crockpot to the eggs and flavorings. Stir back into the rest of tapioca and cook 20 minutes longer. Remove to another bowl and chill. Add whipped cream, if desired. Can make a double batch in a 6 quart crockpot.

Tip: Minute Tapioca or Fine Minute Tapioca my be used to thicken fruit for pies, etc. Use ¼ cup to a quart of liquid.

Tapioca Pudding

3 Tbsp. Minute Tapioca
⅓ c. sugar
dash of salt

1 egg, beaten
2¾ c. milk
¾ tsp. vanilla

Mix together ingredients. Let set 5 minutes. Then bring to a full boil, stirring constantly. Remove from heat. Add vanilla. Stir once after 20 minutes.

Grape Salad

Wilmer & Sarah Beachy

8 oz. cream cheese
1½ c. powdered sugar
1 c. sour cream

1 Tbsp. lemon juice
4 lb. seedless grapes
16 oz. Cool Whip

Beat together first 4 ingredients. Fold in Cool Whip. Add grapes. Yield: Approx. 12 cups.

Cheese Salad

Willard & Carol Ann Helmuth

Bottom Layer:
3 oz. green Jell-O
1¾ c. water

1 c. crushed pineapples (optional)

Middle Layer:
3 oz. orange Jell-O
1½ c. water
8 oz. cream cheese

½ c. sugar
⅔ c. Rich's Topping

Top Layer:
3 oz. red Jell-O

2 c. water

Bottom Layer: Prepare Jell-O. Pour Jell-O and crushed pineapples in bottom of 9"x13" pan. *Middle Layer:* Mix cream cheese with sugar; add to partially set Jell-O. Whip Rich's topping and add to Jell-O and cream cheese. Pour over set bottom layer. *Top Layer:* Mix Jell-O and water. When middle layer is set, pour red Jell-O on top.

Cottage Cheese Salad

Jonathan Lee Miller

3 oz. orange Jell-O
24 oz. cottage cheese
1 sm. can mandarin oranges

1 sm. can crushed pineapples (optional)
2 c. whipped topping

Drain fruit. Mix cottage cheese and dry Jell-O thoroughly. Add fruit and whipped topping. Stir well and serve.

Note: Other Jell-O flavors are also delicious!

Cream Cheese Salad

Anna Viola Beachy

2 c. graham cracker crumbs
½ c. sugar

½ c. butter, melted

Filling:

8 oz. cream cheese, softened
¾ c. powdered sugar

whipped topping
1 can pie filling of your choice

Mix and press in bottom of a 9"x13" pan. Bake at 375° for 8–10 minutes. Cool before adding filling. *Filling:* Mix together cream cheese and powdered sugar; fold in whipped topping. Put on cooled crust and top with pie filling.

Jell-O Salad (12 layer)

Treva Kay Beachy

3 oz. cherry Jell-O
3 oz. lime Jell-O
3 oz. lemon Jell-O
3 oz. orange Jell-O

3 oz. lime Jello
3 oz. strawberry Jell-O
water
2 c. sour cream

Add 1 cup hot water to 3 oz. Jell-O. Take ½ out and add ⅓ cup sour cream. Chill 20 minutes in a 9"x13" pan. Add 3 tablespoons cold water to other ½ of Jell-O. Put together in layers; chill 20 minutes after adding each layer. Repeat with each kind of Jell-O.

Easy Orange Jell-O

Melvin & Beth Ann Beachy

16 oz. cottage cheese
1 sm. can crushed pineapples
1 can mandarin oranges, drained

3 oz. orange Jell-O, dry
9 oz. whipped topping

Combine all ingredients and blend lightly. Refrigerate for several hours.

Orange Sea Salad

Melvin & Beth Ann Beachy

2 lg. box orange Jell-O
8 oz. cream cheese
¾ c. powdered sugar

¾ c. Rich's topping, whipped
fruit (optional)

Mix Jell-O with water according to directions on box. Set aside 2 cups Jell-O. Pour the remaining Jell-O in a 9"x13" pan. When the 2 cups Jell-O is starting to thicken; add cream cheese, powdered sugar, topping and fruit if desired. Mix well. Pour on set Jell-O. Let set again.

Orange Jell-O Salad

Matthew David Miller

12 oz. orange Jell-O
1½ c. whipped topping

11 oz. mandarin oranges
2 c. cottage cheese

Mix Jell-O as directed. You may use juice from oranges for part of cold water. When Jell-O is slightly set whip it well. Add whipped topping, oranges and cottage cheese. Chill until it is set and serve.

Beachy Family Favorites

Ribbon Salad

Levi Beachy Family

Bottom Layer:
6 oz. lime Jell-O
2 c. hot water

2 c. cold water

Middle Layer:
3 oz. lemon Jell-O
1 c. hot water
½ c. miniature marshmallows
1 c. pineapple juice

8 oz. cream cheese
1 can crushed pineapples
1 c. cream, whipped

Top Layer:
6 oz. strawberry Jell-O
2 c. hot water

2 c. cold water

Bottom Layer: Dissolve lime Jell-O in hot water. Add cold water. Pour in a 9"x13" pan. Chill until set. *Middle Layer:* Dissolve lemon Jell-O in hot water in top of double boiler. Add marshmallows and stir to melt. Remove from heat. Add pineapple juice and cream cheese. Beat until blended and stir in pineapples. Cool slightly, until syrupy, then add whipped cream. Pour over lime Jell-O and chill until set. *Top Layer:* Dissolve strawberry Jell-O in 2 cups boiling water. Add 2 cups cold water. Chill until syrupy, then pour over pineapple mixture. Chill until firm. Be sure each layer is set before putting another layer on top.

Sweetheart Salad

Wilmer & Sarah Beachy

7 (3 oz.) boxes lime Jell-O
1½ c. cold water
5 c. crushed pineapples
2 c. sugar
3 c. water

24 oz. cream cheese, softened
1 can Rich's topping
½ c. maraschino cherries
1 c. lemon juice

Dissolve Jell-O in cold water. Add pineapples and sugar to 3 cups water. Bring to boil and add Jell-O. Stir until dissolved. Add lemon and cherry juice. Beat cream cheese and add cherries. Combine with pineapple mixture, a small amount at a time. Chill until slightly thickened. Whip Rich's topping and blend with salad mixture. Mold and chill. Yield: A big batch.

Watergate Salad

Levi & Katie Beachy
Melvin & Beth Ann Beachy

9 oz. whipped topping
1 can crushed pineapples,
   drained

1 c. miniature marshmallows
½ c. chopped nuts
1 box instant pistachio pudding

Fold dry pudding into whipped topping; add the rest of ingredients. Chill and serve.

Cream Cheese Jell-O Salad

Treva Kay Beachy

6 oz. Jell-O, any flavor
8 oz. cream cheese

½ c. sugar
8 oz. Cool Whip

Prepare Jell-O according to directions. Chill until partially set. Mix together cream cheese and sugar; then add topping, beat into Jell-O and chill until firm.

Jell-O Pudding

Orvan & Marilyn Miller

6 oz. Jell-O, any flavor
2½ c. boiling water
4 oz. cream cheese, softened
½ c. sugar

¾ c. sour cream
1¼ c. whipped topping,
    before beating

Dissolve Jell-O in water. Chill until partially set. Beat cream cheese and sugar together until smooth. And sour cream and whipped topping. Add to Jell-O, beat with wire whip until smooth.

Quick and Easy Jell-O

Steven & Lorene Helmuth

6 c. boiling water
6 c. cold milk

2 c. Jell-O, any flavor
1 Tbsp. unflavored gelatin

Mix Jell-O and gelatin together. Add boiling water and mix well. Let cool to lukewarm before adding the cold milk if you want your Jell-O to look like whipped topping is in it. If you want your Jell-O to look like cottage cheese is in it, let the Jell-O cool between hot and lukewarm before adding cold milk. Use a wire whip to mix in the milk.

Whip and Chill Jell-O

Alvin & Charlene Kanagy

1 Tbsp. flour	2 c. water
1 Tbsp. perma-flo	½ c. Jell-O, any flavor
½ c. sugar	9 oz. whip topping

Mix flour, perma-flo, sugar and water; boil together until thickened. Add Jell-O; cool until partly thickened. Mix topping with Jell-O. Refrigerate until set.

Homemade Whipped Topping

Steven & Lorene Helmuth

½ c. boiling water	¾ c. sugar
½ tsp. cream of tartar	1 egg white
1 tsp. vanilla	

Beat until topping stands up in peaks. Good to use in desserts.

Prayer isn't a time to give orders, but a time to report for duty.

Pies

Mom's Apple Pie

Raymond & Martha Beachy

5 lg. apples, peeled, cored and
   sliced in wedges
½ c. sugar
2 Tbsp. flour

2 Tbsp. water
butter
cinnamon

Place apples in unbaked pie shell. Mix together flour, sugar and water; pour over apples. Arrange butter pats on top. Sprinkle with cinnamon. Top with another crust. Make snips in top crust. Sprinkle with sugar. Bake at 350° for 45 minutes or until golden brown.

Thank-You Pie Filling*

Beachy's Bulk Foods

3 c. sugar, divided
1 c. perma-flo, heaping
6 c. water, divided
¾ c. margarine

3 tsp. lemon juice
1 tsp. vanilla
1 tsp. apple pie spice
apples

Mix 1 cup sugar, perma-flo and 1 cup water, set aside. Bring 5 cups water, 2 cups sugar, margarine and lemon juice to a boil, stir in perma-flo mixture and bring to a boil. It needs to be fairly thick. Remove from heat, stir in vanilla, spice and chunked apples, however many you wish. Put in jars; hot water bath for 30 minutes.

Shoestring Apple Pie

Larry Allen Miller

2½ c. sugar
2 Tbsp. flour
3 eggs, well beaten

¼ c. water
4 c. shredded apples
pinch of salt

Mix all together and put in (2) 9" crusts. Sprinkle cinnamon on top. Bake at 325° until done.

Butter Pecan Cream Pie

Rosina Faith Helmuth

2 Tbsp. butter

½ c. pecans

Pie Filling:
6 c. milk
1½ c. brown sugar
2 egg yolks

6 Tbsp. cornstarch
¾ tsp. salt
3 Tbsp. flour

Melt butter until lightly brown; add pecans. Fry on low heat until pecans are lightly brown, set aside. Heat milk to boiling. Mix rest of ingredients and add to milk. Stir and cook until thick. Add 2 teaspoon vanilla and cool. Stir in pecans. Fill 2 baked pie shells. Top with whipped cream and more pecans.

Chocolate Chip Pie

Rebecca & Laura Beachy

6 egg yolks
4 c. milk
3 c. sugar
3 Tbsp. gelatin, dissolved in
   ⅔ c. cold water

1 tsp. vanilla
2 c. whipped topping
3 lg. baked pie shells

Beat egg yolks and milk together in a saucepan; add sugar and heat over medium-low heat for 20 minutes, stirring at all times, do not let boil. Turn off heat, add gelatin which has been soaked, stir until melted and add vanilla. Cool until jelly like, then add 2 cups topping. Fill baked pie shells and top with mini chocolate chips or chocolate shavings right away. These may be frozen.

Note: If using raw milk: heat milk to scalding, cool to refrigerator cold, before using. We like to do this in the evening and then it's ready to use by the next morning. If using store bought milk you don't need to scald it.

Chocolate Fudge Pie

Joseph & Melissa Beachy

¼ c. margarine, melted
1½ c. sugar
3 Tbsp. cocoa

2 eggs, beaten
½ c. milk
1 tsp. vanilla

Mix sugar, cocoa and melted margarine; but do not beat. Stir in eggs and milk a little at a time until all used up. Pour into unbaked pie shell. Bake at 400° for 10 minutes; then at 350° for 25–30 minutes.

Chocolate Mocha Pie

Wilmer & Sarah Beachy

1 Tbsp. unflavored gelatin
¼ c. water
1¼ c. milk
½ c. sugar
1 tsp. instant coffee

1 Tbsp. cocoa
⅛ tsp. salt
1 c. whipped cream
1 tsp. vanilla

Soak gelatin in cold water. Set aside. Combine in saucepan; milk, sugar, coffee, cocoa and salt. Bring to boil, stirring constantly. Add gelatin mixture. Cool until partially set. Beat in vanilla and whipped cream with beater. Pour into baked pie crust. Top with chopped pecans and chocolate syrup.

Chocolate Pie Filling

Treva Kay Beachy

8 c. milk, divided
2 c. sugar
⅔ c. cocoa (scant)
1 c. mira clear

½ tsp. salt
1 Tbsp. vanilla
4 oz. cream cheese

Scald 6 cups milk. Mix dry ingredients with 2 cups milk. Stir into hot milk, boil 1 minute, take off heat and add vanilla and cream cheese. Then cool and use as a pudding or put in baked pie shells and top with whipped topping.

Coconut Cream Pie

Wilmer & Sarah Beachy

2 c. milk, divided
1 egg
⅔ c. sugar
¼ tsp. salt

2 Tbsp. cornstarch, heaping
⅓ c. coconut
1 tsp. coconut flavoring
8 oz. Cool Whip

Heat 1 cup milk with the sugar. Combine remaining 1 cup milk with the egg, salt and cornstarch in blender. Add to saucepan and cook until thickened. Add coconut and flavoring. Cool, covered to prevent skin forming on top. When cool, add 4 oz. Cool Whip. Put into baked pie shell and top with more Cool Whip.

Cranberry Cheese Pie

Wilmer & Sarah Beachy

1 baked pastry shell

Topping:
3 oz. raspberry Jell-O
⅓ c. sugar

1¼ c. cranberry juice
8 oz. can jellied cranberry sauce

Filling:
4 oz. cream cheese, softened
¼ c. sugar
1 Tbsp. milk

1 tsp. vanilla
½ c. whipped topping

Combine Jell-O and sugar. Bring juice to a boil, pour over Jell-O mixture. Stir until dissolved, then stir in cranberry sauce. Chill until slightly thickened. *Filling:* Beat together cream cheese, sugar, milk and vanilla until fluffy. Fold in whipped topping. Spread evenly into pie shell. Beat cranberry topping until frothy, pour over filling. Chill overnight.

Cream Pie Filling

Omer & Dorothy Beachy

6 c. milk, divided
1½ c. sugar, divided
¾ c. perma-flo

6 egg yolks
¼ c. margarine
2 tsp. vanilla

In a saucepan; Combine 5½ cups milk and 1¼ cups sugar; bring to a boil. Mix together perma-flo, ½ cup milk and ¼ cup sugar and egg yolks. Slowly pour this mixture into boiling milk, stirring constantly. When all is added, keep boiling until thickened. Remove from heat and add margarine and vanilla.

Crumb Pie

Abner & Sovilla Mae Zook

8 c. water
2 c. brown sugar
1 c. sugar
2 eggs

5 Tbsp. perma-flo
2 tsp. vanilla
1 tsp. maple flavor

Crumbs:
2½ c. flour
1¼ c. brown sugar
½ c. lard

½ tsp. soda
1 tsp. cream of tartar

Mix together water and sugars; bring to a boil. Add eggs, perma-flo and enough water to make a thin paste. Remove from heat and add vanilla and maple flavoring. Fill unbaked pie shells. Put crumbs on top. Bake at 350°.

Vanilla Crumb Pie

Levi & Katie Beachy

1 c. brown sugar	1 egg
1 c. sugar	1 tsp. vanilla
2 c. water	½ tsp. cream of tartar
2 Tbsp. flour	1 tsp. soda

Crumbs:

2 c. flour	½ tsp. soda
1 c. brown sugar	1 tsp. cream of tartar
½ c. lard	

Boil together first 4 ingredients for 1 minute and set aside. In a larger bowl beat egg, vanilla, cream of tartar and soda. Add to the first syrup mixture, then divide equally into 3 unbaked pie shells. Top with crumbs.

Custard Pie*

Beachy's Bulk Foods

2 c. sugar	3 tsp. vanilla
10 egg yolks	4 c. milk
2 Tbsp. perma-flo, rounded	5 egg whites

Mix ingredients. Fold in 5 stiffly beaten egg whites. Divide evenly into 2 unbaked pie shells. Sprinkle cinnamon on top. Bake at 325° for 1 hour.

Gooseberry Pie Filling

Levi & Katie Beachy

1½ c. sugar
3 c. gooseberries, washed and
   stemmed

3 Tbsp. minute tapioca
¼ tsp. salt
2 Tbsp. butter

Crush ½ cup berries. Combine berries with sugar, tapioca and salt. Cook and stir until thickened and bubbly. Add remaining berries.

Lemon Pie

Marnita Beachy

1½ c. sugar
2 c. water
½ tsp. salt
¼ c. perma-flo, heaping
⅓ c. water

4 egg yolks, slightly beaten
½ c. lemon juice
3 Tbsp. butter
½ tsp. lemon extract

Heat sugar, water and salt to boiling. Mix perma-flo with ⅓ cup water. Add to boiling mixture gradually, stirring constantly. Cook until thickened and clear. Remove from heat. Combine egg yolks, lemon juice and extract, stir into mixture. Return to heat and cook, stirring constantly until mixture bubbles again. Remove from heat, add butter. Cover and cool.

Lemon Chiffon Pie

Melvin & Beth Ann Beachy

9" baked pie shell

4 egg yolks, beaten	1 env. or 1 Tbsp. unflavored
½ c. sugar	gelatin
⅔ c. water	4 egg whites
⅓ c. lemon juice	½ tsp. cream of tartar
	½ c. sugar

Mix egg yolks, ½ cup sugar, water, lemon juice and gelatin in saucepan. Heat just to boiling over medium heat, stirring constantly; remove from heat. Chill, stirring occasionally, until mixture mounds when dropped from a spoon. Beat egg whites and cream of tartar until foamy. Beat in ½ cup sugar, 1 tablespoon at a time; continue beating until stiff and glossy. Do not underbeat. Fold in lemon mixture; mound into pie shell. Refrigerate until set, at least 3 hours. Serve with whip topping. Keep refrigerated.

Lemon Cream Pie Filling

Melvin & Beth Ann Beachy

2 c. sugar	¼ c. ReaLemon
1 lg. box lemon pudding	4½ c. milk, divided
(cook type)	6 egg yolks
⅓ c. flour	1 tsp. lemon flavoring
½ tsp. salt	8 oz. cream cheese

In saucepan, mix sugar, lemon pudding, flour, salt, ReaLemon and 3½ cup milk; mix until smooth. Boil over medium heat. Boil until thickened; remove from heat. Beat egg yolks and 1 cup milk. Gradually add into hot mixture. Bring to boil again until mixture thickens a bit more. Remove from heat; stir in the cream cheese and lemon flavoring. Cool. Put in 2 large baked pie shells. Top with whipped topping.

Beachy Family Favorites

Orange Supreme Pie

Steve & Lorene Helmuth

1 c. sugar
3 Tbsp. clear jel

1 tsp. orange Kool-Aid
3 oranges, peeled and chopped

Bring 1½ cup water to boil; mix together sugar, clear jel and Kool-Aid. Add ½ cup water into sugar mixture and stir. Pour into boiling water, stirring as it cooks. Remove from heat when it begins to thicken a bit. Cool. Stir in orange pieces.

Cream Cheese Mixture for Orange Pie

4 oz. cream cheese
2 c. powdered sugar

8 oz. Cool Whip or
homemade whipped topping

Stir together cream cheese and powdered sugar until creamy. Add Cool Whip. Spoon into baked pie crust. Top with orange filling. May be topped off with extra Cool Whip.

Orange Angel Pie

Wesley & Martha Beachy

3 egg whites, room temp.	dash of salt
¼ tsp. cream of tartar	¾ c. sugar

Filling:

4 egg yolks	¼ c. frozen orange concentrate
1 egg	1 Tbsp. lemon juice
¾ c. sugar	1 c. whipped cream

Combine egg whites, cream of tartar and salt until foamy. Gradually add sugar until stiff. Spread bottom and sides with mixture in well-greased pie pan. Bake at 275° for 1 hour and 10 minutes, let in oven and cool 1 hour. *Filling:* Beat egg yolks and whole egg until lemon color. Beat in sugar, lemon and orange concentrate. Cook until thick, stirring constantly. Fold in whipped cream and put into crust. Chill 12 hours. Put a little Cool Whip on top of pie.

Peach Pie

Alvin & Charlene Kanagy

Crust:
½ c. butter
1 c. flour

3 Tbsp. powdered sugar

Cream Filling:
4 oz. cream cheese

1 can sweetened condensed milk

Peach Filling:
1 c. water
1 c. sugar
3 Tbsp. cornstarch

1 Tbsp. orange or peach Jell-O
peaches, chunked

Crust: Combine butter, flour and powdered sugar. Press into pie pan. *Cream Filling:* Mix ingredients and put in crust. *Peach Filling:* Cook water, sugar, and cornstarch until thickened. Add Jell-O and peaches. Put on top of cream filling.

> *A simple and efficient way to combine flour and a stick of butter for a recipe: Freeze the butter and grate it into the flour and stir a couple of times with a fork.*

Peach Crumb Pie

Landon Zook

7 c. water

½ c. fructose

½ c. perma-flo, heaping

1 c. water

pinch of salt

1 c. orange Jell-O

9 c. peaches

Crumbs:

2 c. flour

1 c. brown sugar

¼ c. sugar

½ tsp. salt

½ c. butter

Boil water and fructose together. Mix perma-flo, water and salt together and stir in the water and sugar mixture and boil. Take off heat and add Jell-O. Add peaches. Sweeten peaches before adding to filling. I use frozen peaches and put them in the hot filling while frozen. *Crumbs:* Mix flour, sugars, salt and butter until crumbly. Put filling in unbaked pie shells. Add crumbs and bake at 350° until nice and brown. Yield: 5–6 pies.

While you prepare a place for us, Lord prepare us for that place.

Peach Pear Pie

Marnita Beachy

⅓ c. brown sugar
¼ c. sugar
3 Tbsp. cornstarch
½ tsp. cinnamon

¼ tsp. allspice
1 Tbsp. lemon juice
2½ c. fresh peaches, sliced
2½ c. fresh pears, sliced

Walnut Streusel:
½ c. flour
¼ c. sugar
3 Tbsp. brown sugar
¼ tsp. cinnamon

¼ tsp. nutmeg
¼ c. cold butter
⅓ c. chopped walnuts

Combine sugars, cornstarch and spices. Sprinkle peaches and pears with lemon juice. Add to dry ingredients, toss to coat. Pour into unbaked pie shell. *Walnut Streusel:* Combine dry ingredients, cut in butter until it resembles coarse crumbs. Stir in nuts. Sprinkle over filling. Cover edges with foil. Bake at 375° for 1 hour or until bubbly. Remove foil.

Pecan Pie

Verna Kay Zook

3 eggs, beaten
¼ c. fructose
1 c. Karo
3 Tbsp. butter

1 tsp. vanilla
dash of salt
1 c. pecans

Melt butter; add all ingredients together. Pour in unbaked pie shell. Bake at 325° until set.

Pecan Pie*

Beachy's Bulk Foods

3 eggs, beaten
½ c. sugar
1 c. light corn syrup
3 Tbsp. butter

1 tsp. vanilla
⅓ tsp. salt
1 c. pecans

Mix well. Pour into an unbaked pie shell. Bake at 350° for 45 minutes.

Cream Cheese Pecan Pie

Lamar Jay Miller

8 oz. cream cheese, softened
½ c. sugar
1 egg, beaten

½ tsp. salt
1 tsp. vanilla
1 c. chopped pecans

Topping:
3 eggs
1 c. light corn syrup

¼ c. sugar
1 tsp. vanilla

Mix together cream cheese, sugar, egg, salt and vanilla; spread into bottom of 9 or 10" unbaked pie shell. Add chopped pecans. *Topping:* Beat until smooth, pour over pecan layer. Bake 35–40 minutes at 375° until golden brown. Delicious!

Mock Pecan Pie

Jonathan Lee Miller

¼ c. butter
¾ c. sugar, white or brown
3 eggs
¾ c. Karo

1 tsp. vanilla
1 c. shredded coconut
¾ c. oatmeal
½ c. pecans (optional)

Cream together butter and sugar. Mix in eggs, Karo and vanilla. Stir in coconut, oatmeal and pecans, if desired. Pour into unbaked 9" pie shell. Bake at 350° for 40–45 minutes.

Not So Rich Pecan Pie

Melvin & Beth Ann Beachy

12 eggs, beaten
5 c. Karo
¾ c. butter, melted
1 c. brown sugar

4 tsp. vanilla
1½ tsp. salt
4 c. chopped pecans

Beat eggs; add Karo, butter, sugar, vanilla and salt. Divide pecans into 4 unbaked pie shells. Divide filling mixture over pecans. Bake at 450° for 10 minutes. Reduce heat to 350° until set. Yield: 4 pies.

Pumpkin Pie

Robert & Dorothy Beachy

2 eggs, beaten
¾ c. sugar
2 Tbsp. flour

1 c. pumpkin
1½ c. milk or cream

Pour into crust. Bake at 350° for 1 hour. Do not cook. Yield: 1 pie.

Pumpkin Pie

Raymond & Martha Beachy

2 eggs, slightly beaten
1½ c. pumpkin
¾ c. sugar
½ tsp. salt

1 tsp. cinnamon
½ tsp. ginger
¼ tsp. cloves
1⅔ c. milk or light cream

Mix together and put into unbaked pie shell. Bake at 350° until set.

Pumpkin Pie*

Beachy's Bulk Foods

4 c. pumpkin
4½ c. sugar
4 eggs, separated
½ c. perma-flo

1 Tbsp. pumpkin pie spice
8 c. milk
pinch of salt

Beat egg yolks, add rest of ingredients. Fold in stiffly beaten egg whites last. Divide evenly into 4 unbaked pie shells. Bake at 350° for 45 minutes or until done.

Pumpkin Cream Pie

Wilmer & Sarah Beachy

1 c. pumpkin
½ c. milk
1 sm. box vanilla instant pudding

3½ c. Rich's whipped topping
4 oz. cream cheese
1 baked crust

Mix cream cheese with a little whipped cream. Spread on crust. Mix together pumpkin, milk, pudding and 2 cups topping; put on top of cream cheese. Put dabs of topping on each piece.

Rhubarb Cream Pie*

Beachy's Bulk Foods

1½ c. sugar
2 eggs, beaten
5 Tbsp. water

1 Tbsp. perma-flo
2 c. chopped rhubarb

Mix together in a bowl. Pour into an unbaked pie shell. Sprinkle with cinnamon. Bake at 350° for 1 hour.

Rhubarb Pie

Wilmer & Sarah Beachy

Filling:
2 c. chopped rhubarb
1 egg, beaten
1 tsp. vanilla

2 Tbsp. flour
½ tsp. salt
1 c. sugar

Crumbs:
¾ c. flour
½ c. brown sugar

¼ c. butter

Mix together filling ingredients. Put in unbaked pie shell. Cover with crumbs. Bake at 425° for 15 minutes. Reduce heat to 350° for 30 minutes or until well baked.

Shoo-Fly Pie

Levi & Katie Beachy

1 c. flour	¾ c. boiling water
⅔ c. brown sugar	1 tsp. soda
1 Tbsp. butter	1 egg, beaten
1 c. dark molasses	

Mix flour, brown sugar and butter into crumbs; set aside half of the mixture. Then mix molasses, water, soda and egg; mix with ½ of crumbs, but do not beat. Put in pie shell and cover with remaining crumbs. Bake at 375° for 11 minutes, then at 350° for 30 minutes.

If you always tell the truth, you never have to remember what you said.

Strawberry Pie

Wilmer & Sarah Beachy

Crust:

1 c. flour

⅓ c. powdered sugar

¼ c. butter, melted

¼ c. chopped nuts

Filling:

1 can sweetened condensed milk

8 oz. cream cheese

2 tsp. lemon juice

Pie Filling:

2 c. water

3 oz. strawberry Jell-O

½ c. sugar

2 Tbsp. perma-flo, heaping

¼ c. water

pinch of salt

1 qt. fresh strawberries

Crust: Mix ingredients and press into 9" pie pan. Bake at 350° until golden brown (will burn easily). Cool. *Filling:* Mix ingredients and spread on crust. Refrigerate until firm. *Pie Filling:* Bring water, strawberry Jell-O and sugar to a boil; add perma-flo, water and salt. Mix together before adding to boiling mixture. Cool, then add fresh strawberries. Top pie with strawberry filling. Garnish with whipped topping.

Strawberry Pie Filling

Abner & Sovilla Mae Zook

3½ c. water

⅔ c. (6 oz.) strawberry Jell-O

½ c. sugar

¼ c. perma-flo

½ c. water

pinch of salt

Bring water, strawberry Jell-O and sugar to a boil; add perma-flo, water and salt. Let cool until thickened, then add strawberries as desired.

Chocolate Pie Crust

Steve & Lorene Helmuth

1¼ c. sifted flour
⅓ c. sugar
¼ c. cocoa
½ tsp. salt

½ c. shortening
½ tsp. vanilla
2–3 Tbsp. cold water

Mix dry ingredients. Cut in shortening; add vanilla. Sprinkle with water. Form a ball, roll out. Press into pie pan. Bake. Fill crust with peanut butter pudding, (or any kind of pudding is delicious!). Top with whip topping and peanut butter crumbs.

Pie Crust

Willard & Carol Ann Helmuth

5¾ c. flour
2½ c. Crisco

1 tsp. salt

Combine flour, Crisco and salt; after it's all crumbly, add 1 tablespoon vinegar in a cup and fill up with cold water. Then add to crumbs and stir until moistened, but do not overmix. Do not get too dry with flour. Yield: 8–9 crusts.

Commercial Pie Dough*

Beachy's Bulk Foods

2 c. pie dough improver
5 lb. flour
3 lb. + 1 c. Crisco
2⅞ c. water
2 Tbsp. vinegar

2 eggs
4 tsp. salt
4 tsp. sugar
4 tsp. baking powder

Mix together dry ingredients. Then mix with Crisco until you have fine crumbs. Mix together water, eggs and vinegar, beat well. Pour this into Crisco mixture and mix with hands until crumbs are well moistened. Try not to overmix.

Flaky Pie Crust Mix

Melvin & Beth Ann Beachy

Pie Crust Mix:
12½ c. flour
5 c. vegetable shortening

2 Tbsp. salt

To Use Mix:
2½ c. pie crust mix
1 egg

¼ c. cold water
1 Tbsp. white vinegar

Pie Crust Mix: Mix; store in an airtight container.

Never Fail Pie Crust*

Beachy's Bulk Foods

4 c. flour
1 tsp. salt
1 Tbsp. sugar
1 tsp. baking powder
1¾ c. Crisco or 1½ c. lard

½ c. cold water
1 egg, well beaten
1 tsp. vinegar
⅓ c. pie dough improver
(optional)

Mix together flour, salt, sugar, baking powder and pie dough improver. Mix with Crisco until you have very fine crumbs. Mix together water, vinegar and beaten egg. Pour this into Crisco mixture and mix until crumbs are well moistened. Try not to overmix.

Fry Pie Dough

Melvin & Beth Ann Beachy

9 c. cake flour
2 c. water
shortening
2 Tbsp. sugar

1 tsp. salt
3 c. B.B.S. or Creme Tex

Glaze:
4 lb. powdered sugar
¼ c. cornstarch
⅓ c. Carnation milk

½ tsp. vanilla
2⅛ c. water

Mix like pie dough. Roll out thin and cut a circle the size you want your pie. Wet edges and place the pie filling of your choice in center of circle, fold over and crimp edges. Deep fat fry in B.B.S. or Creme Tex shortening at 380°–400° until slightly brown. When cooled, dip in glaze and place on wire rack to drip. These are best when fresh. When storing, don't cover tightly as they get soggy. Yield: 40–60 depending on size.

Canning & Freezing

Apple Butter

Raymond & Martha Beachy

Fill 33 quart cooker ¾ full with Jonathan apples; add 15 lbs. sugar, then fill cooker heaping full with apples. Let set overnight. In the morning add 1⅓ quarts of water. Cook 3–4 hours until apples look glossy. Then add 2 heaping tablespoons of cinnamon and a scant 2 tablespoons allspice. Put through Victoria Strainer and put in jars and seal. Cold pack until water is boiling.

Apple Butter

Steve & Lorene Helmuth

1 gal. applesauce
3 lb. brown sugar
1 c. vinegar or water
1 tsp. cinnamon
½ tsp. allspice
½ tsp. cloves
½ c. Red Hots (optional)

Mix together in roaster and bake at 350° for 3 hours or to suit your taste. Stir occasionally. If I use old presweetened applesauce, I cut back on sugar.

The greatest remedy for anger is delay.

Apple Butter

Jonathan Lee Miller

2 gal. apples, cored and cut in
   fourths, unpeeled
5 lb. sugar
1 pt. water

1 tsp. cinnamon
½ tsp. allspice
½ tsp. cloves

Core apples in evening, put in stockpot and add sugar and water. Let set overnight. Boil 3 hours (without lifting lid). Have burner on low. Work through Victoria Strainer, then add spices. Mix well. Put in jars and hot water bath 15–20 minutes.

Elderberry or Garden Huckleberry Jam

Raymond & Martha Beachy

1½ c. juice
1½ c. water
¼ c. lemon juice

⅓ c. pectin
2 lb. sugar

Bring first 4 ingredients to a boil. Add sugar and bring to a full rolling boil. Boil for 1 minute.

Mulberry Jelly

Levi & Katie Beachy

8 c. mulberry juice
⅔ c. Pen Jel

11 c. sugar
½ c. lemon

Heat juice, put in Pen Jel and melt; add sugar and lemon juice when in a full boil, cook 2 minutes, put in jars and seal.

Pear Honey

Levi & Katie Beachy

10 c. crushed pears   14 c. sugar
5 c. crushed pineapples   3 boxes Pen Jel

Cook pears, drain and crush. Add pineapples and Pen Jel. Heat to boiling, then add sugar. Boil 45 minutes. Put in jars and seal.

Rhubarb Jam

Levi & Katie Beachy

5 c. finely cut rhubarb   6 oz. strawberry Jell-O
4 c. sugar

Boil rhubarb and sugar together for 5 minutes. Remove from heat and stir in Jell-O until dissolved. Pour in jars and seal. May hot water bath for 10 minutes, if you prefer.

Barbecue Sauce to Can

Orvan & Marilyn Miller

4 qt. ketchup   2 Tbsp. garlic powder
3 c. brown sugar   1 Tbsp. white pepper
⅓ c. Liquid Smoke   ⅓ c. mustard
⅓ c. Worcestershire sauce

Use your favorite ketchup recipe or you can also use Mrs. Wages ketchup mix and make ketchup. Then add rest of ingredients. Mix well. Ladle into jars and process 10 minutes in hot water bath.

Ketchup

Orvan & Marilyn Miller

4 qt. tomato juice	½ tsp. red pepper
2 Tbsp. salt	2 c. vinegar
1 Tbsp. cinnamon, scant	1 Tbsp. mixed pickling spice
1 tsp. ground mustard	3 sm. onions
3 c. sugar	

Put pickling spice and onions in bag. Cook 20 minutes. Remove bag and thicken. Put in cans and hot water bath 10 minutes.

Ketchup

Lamar Jay Miller

1 gal. tomato juice	2 Tbsp. salt
4 c. sugar	1½ c. vinegar
2 sm. onions	2 Tbsp. cinnamon
(cook whole with juice)	

Cook 2 hours on low heat. Thicken to desired thickness with perma-flo. Put in jars and process 15 minutes in hot water bath.

The best way for a housewife to have a few minutes to herself is to start doing the dishes.

Tomato Ketchup

Abner & Sovilla Mae Zook

4 qt. tomato juice
2½ c. vinegar
2 c. fructose
¼ c. salt
1 onion

½ tsp. cinnamon
½ tsp. ginger
½ tsp. cloves
½ tsp. nutmeg
½ tsp. cayenne pepper

Boil several hours, then thicken with 1 cup perma-flo and ½ cup water. The longer you boil it, the less perma-flo it takes. Canning time: 35 minutes.

Pizza Sauce

Raymond & Martha Beachy

4 qt. tomato juice
8 tsp. basil
4 tsp. oregano
4 tsp. salt
3 slices Velveeta cheese

1 Tbsp. pepper
4 tsp. garlic salt
½ Tbsp. Tabasco sauce
¾ c. brown sugar
½ c. butter

Mix all ingredients to simmer or until desired thickness. Pour into jars and process 20–25 minutes. Thicken with perma-flo.

Salsa

Raymond & Martha Beachy

5 lb. tomatoes, washed, peeled, cored and chopped (about 8 c.)
2 c. chopped onions
1½ c. seeded and chopped jalapeño peppers
⅔ c. lemon juice
3 Tbsp. fresh cilantro (I use dried)
2½ tsp. salt

Combine all ingredients in a 6 quart kettle. Bring to a boil; reduce heat. Boil gently, uncovered for 30 minutes, stirring occasionally. Spoon into hot jars, leaving ½" headspace. Hot water bath for 15 minutes.

Vegetable Juice Cocktail

Orvan & Marilyn Miller

1 qt. cut-up carrots
1 qt. cut-up celery
2 c. chopped onions
1 pepper, chopped
2 beets (optional)
8 qt. tomato juice
¼ c. salt
2 c. sugar

Cook carrots, celery, onions and pepper in tomato juice until soft. Put through Victoria Strainer. Put in jars and hot water bath 10–15 minutes. Delicious to drink. Use as regular tomato juice, it will add a good flavor.

Corn to Freeze

Orvan & Marilyn Miller

8 c. corn (cut off cob)	2 Tbsp. sugar
1 c. water	1 Tbsp. salt

Put corn in 6 or 8 quart kettle. Heat to boil. Remove from heat immediately and place in cold water. When chilled put in container and freeze. Add a dab of butter when fixing for a meal.

Corn to Freeze

Orvan & Marilyn Miller

Large Recipe:	*Small Recipe:*
15 c. corn	10 c. corn
¾ c. sugar	½ c. sugar
5 tsp. salt	3⅓ tsp. salt
4 c. ice water	2⅔ c. ice water

Cut corn off cobs. No blanching. Mix together water, sugar and salt. Pour over corn and mix again. (For extra sweet variety of corn, use less sugar.) Put in containers and freeze. When ready to use, heat to boiling and boil for 2 minutes. Add a dash of butter.

Fruit to Can

Orvan & Marilyn Miller

4 c. fruit purée, blackberry,
  black raspberry, grape
4 c. water

2 c. sugar
½ tsp. salt
2½ c. perma-flo

Heat fruit, water, sugar and salt to boiling. Mix perma-flo with water. Use enough water so you have like a thin gravy. Mix perma-flo and water into fruit, stirring constantly. Return to boiling, then remove from heat.

Freezing Peaches

Renita Faye Helmuth

1 sm. can frozen orange juice
  concentrate

4 c. sugar
3 c. water

Mix together thoroughly and slice peaches into juice. Ladle into containers to freeze. Continue to slice peaches into juice until all used up. Delicious!

Corn Relish

Wesley & Martha Beachy

24 ears corn
3 single stems celery
3 onions
6 peppers
1 head cabbage

1 c. vinegar
2 c. sugar
1 c. water
2 Tbsp. salt
1 tsp. mustard

Cut corn off cob. Chop celery, onions, peppers and cabbage. Mix together. Heat brine and put vegetables in. Cook slowly for 15 minutes. Put in jars and seal.

Pickle Relish*

Beachy's Bulk Foods

1 gal. ground pickles
1 pt. ground onions
6 c. sugar
3 tsp. mustard seed

3 c. vinegar
3 tsp. celery seed
2 tsp. turmeric

Soak pickles and onions in salt water for 2 hours, then drain. Add rest of ingredients. Heat to boiling. Turn burner on low and boil for 30 minutes. Put in jars and seal.

Pepper Relish*

Beachy's Bulk Foods

12 green peppers
12 red peppers
12 onions
12 green tomatoes

3 c. vinegar
3 c. sugar
3 Tbsp. salt

Grind peppers and onions together. Grind tomatoes separately. Pour enough boiling water over ground peppers and onions to cover. Let set 5 minutes, then drain. Bring vinegar, sugar and salt to a boil; add to ground vegetables and cook all together for 10 minutes. Put in jars and seal.

Banana Pickles

Orvan & Marilyn Miller

2½ c. sugar
1 c. vinegar
1 c. water
1 tsp. salt

1 tsp. celery seed
1 tsp. mustard seed
1 tsp. turmeric

Peel pickles. Cut in half. If large pickles, scoop seeds out. Can either cut in spears or cut ¾" slices crosswise. Pack in jars. Cover with vinegar mixture. Cold pack for 5 minutes after water boils.

Freezer Pickles

Melvin & Beth Ann Beachy

7 c. cucumbers
1 c. peppers (optional)
1 c. onions
1 Tbsp. salt

1 tsp. celery seed
2 c. sugar
1 c. white vinegar

Mix all together and let set in ice box 1 day, stir occasionally, put in containers and freeze.

A good cook always adds a pinch of love.

Spicy Frozen Cucumbers

Raymond & Martha Beachy

4 c. pickling cucumbers,
  3–4" long, washed, unpeeled
  and thinly sliced
2 lg. onions, peeled and
  thinly sliced

1 Tbsp. salt
1 c. sugar
½ c. cider vinegar
1 Tbsp. whole white mustard seeds
½ tsp. ground turmeric

Combine the cucumbers, onions and salt in a large glass or ceramic bowl. Let set for 2–4 hours to extract moisture. Rinse the vegetables well, blotting them with paper towels to absorb all moisture. Combine the remaining ingredients and mix well until sugar is completely dissolved, about 10 minutes. Stir in cucumbers and onions. Pour cucumber mixture into freezer containers, leaving 1" space for expansion. Cap and seal. Will keep up to 1 year in freezer. To use thaw about 4 hours in refrigerator. Serve chilled.

Canning Beets

Levi & Katie Beachy

3 c. vinegar
3 c. sugar

6 c. water
1½ tsp. salt

Leave your grate or rack in your pressure cooker and fill ⅔ full of beets. Add 4 quarts water. Cook at 10 lbs. pressure for 15 minutes for small beets and 20 minutes for large beets. When beets are cooled enough to handle, peel and dice. Fill cans with beets and juice (this recipe) leaving 1" headspace. Hot water bath for 15 minutes.

This 'n That

Bratwurst

Raymond & Martha Beachy

10 lb. ground pork
3 eggs
2 c. milk
1 Tbsp. white pepper

1 Tbsp. mace
1 tsp. ginger
1 Tbsp. nutmeg
5 Tbsp. salt

Mix well and stuff in casings. Freeze.

Breakfast Sausage Seasoning Mix

Orvan & Marilyn Miller

fresh ground pork

For 25 lbs.:	For 10 lbs.:
⅔ c. salt	¼ c.
2½ Tbsp. white pepper	1 Tbsp.
¼ c. rubbed sage	1½ Tbsp. (optional)
2½ tsp. ginger	1 tsp.
2½ Tbsp. nutmeg	1 Tbsp.
2½ Tbsp. thyme	1 Tbsp.
5 c. ice water	2 c.
2½ Tbsp. hot red pepper	1 Tbsp. (optional)

Mix together and stuff into casings or make patties to fry.

Tennessee Sausage Seasonings

Orvan & Marilyn Miller

10 lb. ground pork	1 tsp. red pepper (I use ¾ tsp.)
⅓ c. salt	mustard seed (optional)
¼ c. ginger, scant	or 1½ tsp. ground mustard
2 tsp. white pepper	or 3 tsp. honey mustard

Mix together and stuff into casings or make patties to fry. This recipe is also good to make meatballs to can. Cover with pork broth.

Deer Sausage

Raymond & Martha Beachy

25 lb. ground deer meat	½ c. salt
3 lb. bacon	3 Tbsp. black pepper
3 lb. sausage	1 Tbsp. red pepper
½ c. Liquid Smoke	

Grind deer meat and bacon once, then add rest of ingredients. Mix all meat and seasoning well and grind again. Package and freeze or may be canned.

Deer Sausage

Melvin & Beth Ann Beachy

25 lb. ground deer meat	1 Tbsp. red pepper
5 lb. bacon	3 Tbsp. black pepper
20 lb. sausage, seasoned with	½ c. salt
salt and pepper	½ c. Liquid Smoke

Grind all together and mix well. Fry as for burgers.

Chicken Bologna

Treva Kay Beachy

75 lb. ground meat
2 lb. Tender Quick
1½ lb. brown sugar
4 tsp. black pepper

3 qt. water
1 Tbsp. garlic powder
1 Tbsp. salt petre
2 Tbsp. Liquid Smoke

Mix all together and pack in jars. Water bath for 3 hours.

Chicken Bologna

Abner & Sovilla Mae Zook

25 lb. fresh chicken
1½ c. Tender Quick
1 oz. black pepper
½ c. sugar

2 tsp. garlic salt
3 Tbsp. Liquid Smoke
3 c. water

Chill chicken 24 hours. Grind chicken meat. Add all ingredients and mix well. Grind again. Put in jars and cook 3 hours. Slice and eat!

Note: Turkey meat may also be used.

Peroxide or 7-Up helps to get blood stains out of clothes.

Ham Recipe

Orvan & Marilyn Miller

50 lb. pork
1 lb. Tender Quick
9 Tbsp. Liquid Smoke
10 oz. honey
1⅓ c. brown sugar

4 oz. or 10 Tbsp. sodium
    phosphate (we use cornstarch)
6 Tbsp. black pepper
3½ tsp. red pepper
4 qt. water

Grind pork. Mix in seasoning. Grind again. Let set 3 days. Grind again and stuff in bags (I sew bags from new flat sheets.) Close bag with twist tie. Wrap in heavy aluminum foil. Bake at 200° until internal temperature is 155°. This takes around 6 hours.

Pork Bologna

Larry Allen Miller

25 lb. ground meat (pork)
¾ lb. Tender Quick
2 c. brown sugar
1½ Tbsp. black pepper
1 tsp. salt petre (optional)

1½ tsp. garlic powder
1 lb. powdered milk
5 tsp. Liquid Smoke
1 qt. water

Grind together meat and Tender Quick and mix, then let set 24–48 hours. Mix rest of ingredients with meat, then stuff in cloth bags. Wrap with heavy duty aluminum foil. Bake at 170° for 6–7 hours. Meat is done when internal temperature is 155°. Cool immediately! (Grind meat 4 times).

Turkey Bologna
Orvan & Marilyn Miller

25 lb. meat	1 tsp. mace
½ lb. Tender Quick	½ lb. cornstarch
½ tsp. salt petre	2½ qt. water
1 Tbsp. white pepper	3 Tbsp. Liquid Smoke (optional)
1 Tbsp. coriander	

Mix together. Grind meat fine. Let set for 4 days. Stuff into cans. Hot water bath for 2½ hours or pressure can 1½ hours at 10 lb. pressure.

Note: We buy the ground turkey at the store, and also some breasts. We usually ratio to 20 lb. turkey and 5 lbs. breasts.

Venison Summer Sausage
Raymond & Martha Beachy

24 lb. ground venison	1 c. Tender Quick
¼ c. mustard powder	4 Tbsp. Liquid Smoke
3 Tbsp. black pepper (heaping)	2 Tbsp. onion salt (heaping)
2 Tbsp. garlic salt (heaping)	6 c. water

Mix all well. Cover and refrigerate. Mix every day for 3 days. (We just let set for 3 days then grind again.) On the 4th day form into compact 2", 1 lb. rolls. Place on oven racks, allowing grease to drip off. Cover entire bottom of oven with foil to catch drippings. Bake at 350° for 1–1½ hours. Turn rolls after 30 minutes. Cool, wrap in saran wrap and freezer paper to freeze. Can also be put in 2" casings and baked.

Beachy Family Favorites

To Soak Tenderloin or Ribs

Orvan & Marilyn Miller

10 lb. cut tenderloin
⅓ c. salt, scant
2 tsp. soda

⅓ c. brown sugar, rounded
2 tsp. Liquid Smoke
water, enough to cover meat

Bring water to a boil, then let cool before putting in meat. Let soak 1 week, wash in clear water. Freeze or bake.

Noodles*

Beachy's Bulk Foods

2 c. egg yolks
⅔ c. water

¾ tsp. yellow food coloring
8 c. flour

Mix well, making a very stiff dough. Roll out thin and cut in strips and lay on sheet to dry for 3 days.

Easy Homemade Noodles

Raymond & Martha Beachy

Put enough flour in plastic bowl to weigh 4 lbs. including bowl. Beat egg yolks from 3 dozen eggs (at least 2 cups) with 1½ cups boiling water, until foamy. Make sure the water is boiling hot, then beat quickly. Now pour this mixture into flour, stir with a large fork until stiff. May need to add more flour, dough should not be sticky. Shape into a ball. Put in plastic bag and let set 10–30 minutes. Knead a little bit and it is ready for the noodlemaker.

Cinnamon Butter

Delmer Helmuth

1 c. butter
¼ c. powdered sugar

1 Tbsp. honey
2 tsp. cinnamon

Mix all together. Spread on bread instead of jam or jelly.

Church Peanut Butter

Levi Beachy Family

3 c. brown sugar
3 c. water
2 c. butter

5 lb. peanut butter
1 gal. marshmallow creme
1 c. Karo

Boil together sugar and water. Melt butter in that. Mix in rest of ingredients. Cool. This will be thin until it is cooled.

Peanut Butter Spread *

Beachy's Bulk Foods

2 lb. peanut butter
6 oz. marshmallow creme

2 c. Karo

Mix together and spread on bread.

Church Spread

Lamar Jay Miller

1 c. jam or jelly, strawberry,
 blackberry or your choice
1 c. powdered sugar

½ c. butter
8 oz. cream cheese

Soften cream cheese and butter. Add powdered sugar and jam. Beat real well. Chill and enjoy!

Cheese Spread

Levi Beachy Family

1 lb. Velveeta cheese
1¼ lb. American cheese

2⅔ c. milk
½ c. margarine

Melt together in 275°–300° oven, stirring occasionally. Cool. Use for spread on bread.

Velveeta Cheese

Raymond & Martha Beachy

1 gal. milk
3 tsp. citric acid
¾ tsp. soda
¼ c. butter

1½–2 tsp. salt or to suit taste
3 Tbsp. cheddar cheese powder
3 oz. milk

Heat 1 gallon milk to 140°. Remove from heat and add citric acid; 1 teaspoonful at a time. Stir gently until separated; drain off whey. To curds add; soda, butter, salt, cheddar cheese powder and 3 oz. milk or less (depends on how you want your cheese.) (I usually add 5 oz. for 2 recipes for slicing.) Heat together and stir briskly until lumps dissolve. Put in container to set. Refrigerate.

Yogurt

Raymond & Martha Beachy

1 gal. goats milk
2 c. sugar, rounded
2 Tbsp. vanilla
½ c. creamer

10 tsp. gelatin
⅔ c. cold water
½–¾ c. plain yogurt

Soak gelatin in cold water, set aside. Heat milk to 180°; add sugar, vanilla, creamer and soaked gelatin. Cool milk to 110° and add plain yogurt. Put in glass quart jars and cap tightly. Let set in oven (with oven off) for 4–6 hours. The more yogurt you add and the longer you let it set the tarter it gets. For flavored yogurt add 1 teaspoon Jell-O per quart. Refrigerate until thick.

Yogurt

Steven & Lorene Helmuth

1 gal. milk
2 Tbsp. gelatin in
　½ c. cold water
1 c. sugar

1 Tbsp. vanilla
¼ c. plain yogurt
⅓ c. Jell-O, any flavor

Heat milk to 190°. Meanwhile soak the gelatin in cold water. Add to milk when 190°; beat well. Let cool until 160° (works best or 150° would too). Then add sugar, vanilla and yogurt. Beat well, very well or it will be lumpy. Then add your Jell-O. Put in jars with lids. Put in oven (not turned on) for 6–7 hours. Refrigerate. *To Make Philadelphia Cream Cheese:* Instead of refrigerating when yogurt has formed, pour into thick cloth, catch whey, by dripping for 1 minute. Tie together 4 ends of cloth; hang on faucet to let whey drip about 8 hours. When ready remove from bag and store in refrigerator. Yield: Approx. 8 oz.

Vanilla Ice Cream

Steven & Lorene Helmuth

6 c. milk
3 c. sugar
¾ c. cornstarch
½ tsp. salt
1½ pkg. Knox gelatin

6 egg yolks
6 c. thick cream or milk
1½ tsp. vanilla
6 egg whites, beaten

Scald milk and add sugar, cornstarch and salt which have been blended in 1 cup cold milk. Cook until thick. Add the egg yolks which have been mixed with 3 tablespoons of milk. Cool 1 minute. Add gelatin mixture which has been soaked in 3 tablespoons of cold milk. Remove cooked custard from stove and let cool. Then add the cream, vanilla and well beaten egg whites. Freeze. Yield: 1½ gallon.

Always do right—this will gratify some people and astonish others.

Ice Cream Bars

Steve & Lorene Helmuth

Crumbs:

2 c. graham cracker crumbs
¼ c. sugar

½ c. margarine

Filling:

2 Tbsp. cocoa
½ c. sugar
1½ c. milk
6 eggs, separated

⅓ c. sugar
¼ tsp. salt
¾ c. sugar
2 c. cream, whipped

Crumbs: Mix ingredients and put half of mixture in bottom of cake pan. *Filling:* Mix cocoa, ½ cup sugar and milk; bring to scalding. Add well beaten egg yolks to which ⅓ cup sugar has been added. Cook until slightly thick. Cool. Beat the 6 egg whites, add the salt and ¾ cup sugar until they are glossy and stiff. Add to cooled mixture. Also add 2 cups cream, whipped. Place in cake pan on top of crumbs. Sprinkle remaining crumbs on top. Cover and freeze until firm. To serve, cut into bars.

Chocolate Syrup

Larry Allen Miller

4 c. brown sugar
4 c. sugar
2 c. cocoa

½ c. light Karo
3 c. water
½ Tbsp. vanilla

Mix all ingredients except vanilla in an 8 quart kettle. Bring to a boil and boil 5 minutes. Remove from heat. Add vanilla. Pour in jars and seal. Use to make chocolate milk, drizzle over ice cream or use in recipes. If too thick, add water.

A Midnight Camping Snack

Renita Helmuth

1 bag lg. marshmallow
1 lg. bag Hersheys candy bars
(any kind you like)

1 box Ritz or graham crackers

Gather sticks and make a bonfire. When burned down, roast marshmallows. Gather chairs and sit together, to visit, sing, and etc. When marshmallows are roasted (do not burn or blacken them) put between crackers with a bite-size candy bar. A favorite midnight snack when camping, LOADED with calories!

Never Fail Marshmallows

Raymond & Martha Beachy

4 env. plain gelatin
1 c. water, divided
2 c. sugar
½ c. light corn syrup

1½ tsp. vanilla
2 eggs, stiffly beaten
powdered sugar

Dissolve gelatin in ½ cup water. Boil remaining water with sugar, syrup and vanilla until it reaches a softball stage. Remove from heat; add gelatin. Beat until cool and white. Add egg whites, beat for 5 minutes. Turn out into pan, generously dusted with powdered sugar. When set cut into squares with sharp knife dipped in cold water, roll squares in powdered sugar.

Cream Of Chicken Soup

Orvan & Marilyn Miller

3 Tbsp. butter, melted   ¼ tsp. salt
3 Tbsp. flour   pepper
1 c. milk   pinch of Lawry's seasoned salt

Mix together butter and flour. Then add milk, salt, pepper, Lawry's seasoned salt. Add bits of chicken and chicken base for cream of chicken soup. For cream of mushroom soup, add beef base and chopped mushrooms. Yield: 1 (10¾ oz.) can.

Tartar Sauce

Melvin & Beth Ann Beachy

1 qt. salad dressing   ½ tsp. salt
1 c. pepper relish or pickle relish   1½ tsp. mustard
2 Tbsp. sugar

Mix all together. This is good on fish.

Deep Fat Fry Batter

Melvin & Beth Ann Beachy

1 c. flour   1 egg
1 tsp. baking powder   ¼ c. vegetable oil
½ tsp. salt   1 c. milk

For corn dogs, add ½ cup cornmeal.

For Tomato Blight

Raymond & Martha Beachy

1 gal. water
1 Tbsp. salt petre
1 Tbsp. baking powder

1 Tbsp. Epsom salt
1 tsp. ammonia

Mix well and give 1 pint of this to each plant, every two weeks. Start early in the spring and quit once the plants have fairly big and green tomatoes on them. This seems to fertilize too. Give this after 5 p.m.

Ear Drops

Raymond & Martha Beachy

2 c. olive oil
½ c. chopped onions

½ c. chopped garlic

Combine ingredients in the top of double boiler and heat over boiling water for 2 hours. DO NOT allow the oil to boil. Strain the infused oil and store in a cool dark place. I sometimes use mullein if I have some, but I have already made it without and it worked fine. If you use mullein, replace equal amounts of onion and garlic. Warm oil before using and use a few drops in each ear for earache and ear infection.

Play Dough
Lavon Dean Helmuth

½ c. salt
1 c. flour
2 Tbsp. cream of tartar
1 c. boiling water

1 Tbsp. vegetable oil
a few drops flavoring (optional)
food coloring, any color you want

Mix together until lump free. Store in airtight container and keep in cool place. Use within 6 months or dough will get sticky.

Play Dough
JoAnna Sue Miller

2¾ c. flour
½ c. salt
3 Tbsp. vegetable oil

1 Tbsp. alum
2 c. boiling water
food coloring

Stir together. Children will play many creative hours with this. This will keep several months if stored in an airtight container and in a cool place.

Silly Putty
Lavon Dean Helmuth

3 c. warm water, divided
2 c. Elmer's glue

3 tsp. Borax

Mix 1½ cup warm water and glue together. Add remaining water and Borax. Mix, using your hands.

Soap Bubble

Lavern Andrew Helmuth

1 part liquid detergent   5 parts water
1 part glycerin

Makes a generous supply! Put in small dish and use an empty bottle to blow bubbles. Put in small bottles for later use.

Wet Ones

Orvan & Marilyn Miller

2 c. hot water   2 Tbsp. soap
2 Tbsp. baby oil   paper towel roll

Cut paper towel roll in half. Remove cardboard from paper towels. (Viva or Bounty work best.) Put in container and pour water mixture over paper towels. Any hand soap or shampoo will work, but Shaklee Basic H works best for me. It doesn't get so smelly.

Windex

Steve & Lorene Helmuth

½ c. rubbing alcohol   7½ c. warm water
½ c. ammonia   a couple drops blue food coloring

Mix well.

Recipe for a Boiled Wife

Take one cool, fresh, good-natured wife. Add 3 small children, a yelping dog and a cranky neighbor. Stir well! Blend in equal parts of heat, humidity, dust, and stale air. Baste with annoying interruptions, spilled milk, skinned knees, washing that won't wait, a big ironing to do, a counter piled high with dishes and jelly smeared all over the floor. Top with a splitting headache; let simmer in a 98° home for 10 hours or until boiling point is reached.

A Favorite Recipe

Take a cup of Kindness
Mix it well with Love
Add a lot of Patience
And Faith in God above
Sprinkle very generously
With Joy and Thanks and Cheer
And you'll have lots of Angel Food
To feast on all the year.

Recipe for Child Rearing

1 cup Proverbs 22:6
2 Tbsp. Proverbs 19:18
A dash of Proverbs 22:1-8

A pinch of Ephesians 6:4
½ cup of Titus 2:3-7

Mix all ingredients; add a pound of persistence, 1 cup of Love. Stir together until the right consistency. This recipe is recommended by the Creator of mankind.

Note: Look it up, you'll find it interesting.

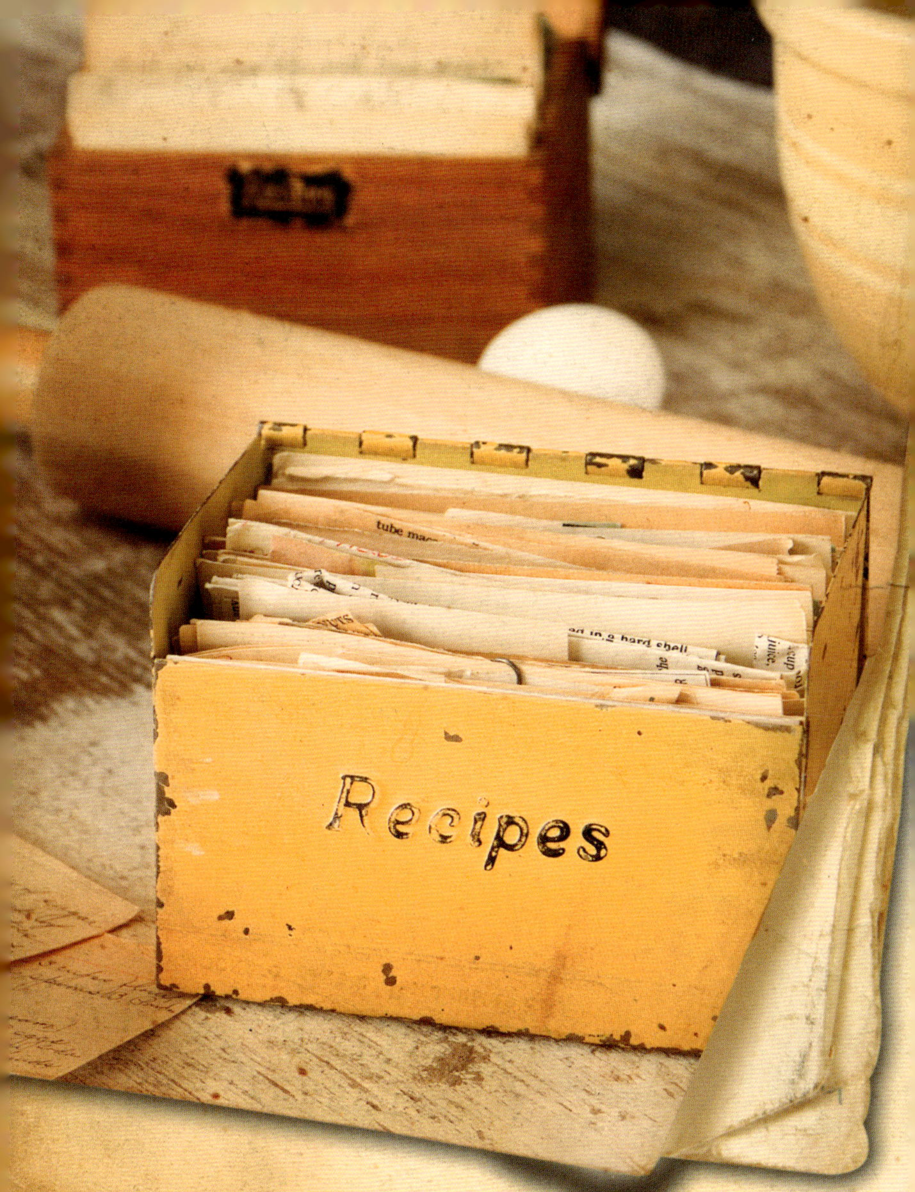

Index

Beachy Family Favorites

Salad, Soup, & Sandwiches

Meats & Main Dishes

Beachy Family Favorites

Index

Beachy Family Favorites